Paper Highway
The Collected Works

Poetry, Prose & Cosmic Commentary

J.D. Howard

This work is a compilation of original poetry, prose, social commentary and political satire. All rights are reserved. No part of this publication shall be reproduced without the written consent of the author. All chapter symbols acquired from the public domain. By-line quotes used by permission.

Author Photo: Susan Harrell
Editing: Skyler Cuthill
Cover: Matthew Morse

paper.highway.jdhoward@gmail.com

Son Earth Publishing
Copyright © 2020 by JD Howard
ISBN: 978-1-7336043-2-1

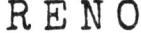

*Every artist starts with his own palette
then paints the reality of his soul*

WHIMSY

Any belief that all art is serious is . . . an illusion

Everyone Needs Art

Egyptian blue
Sierra gold
With just a Touch of Grey

Colors bold
Shades of life
The beauty comes my way

Dreams in vivid
Chimera sleep
A hint of reverie

Wash over me
In floods of deep
Soak my soul until I'm clean

The sands of life
Are running out
Where is thy victory

Still yet un-won
I battle on
Till silence comes over me

Let's talk of epitaphs
Anecdotes and quotes
I've ended before I start

With fist slammed down
I hereby state — Everyone Needs Art!

2008

Such is Life

All the ideas
Have left the room
The talent's all gone
We peaked too soon

Like a high water wave
Crest at high noon
Little Wing has flown
The Skeleton too

We flew until
Our souls were burnin'
But bring it back to me
I'm not finished learnin'

Still chasin' that feelin'
Around every bend
The circle the cycle
It's not quite the end

Fill me up
Drink the cup
Such is life
There's never enough

2006

The Gift

Bring me the gift
Of crashing salt water
Show me the love
In bold color of leaves

To be with the music
The spirit that guides
Notes on the sunset
Song on the tide

Wind on Gardner Bay
Waves hit the shore

       Encore!

            Encore!

Fall 1972

Carnival Incident

There were wares for sale
        Chicken coops too

Mary Jones
        Was in the kissing booth
                She's a capitalist!

Tennessee Jed was in the corner
        Picking tunes
On a guitar
        With glasses on
                And a raven on his shoulder

Dr. Zeno and Mr. Doom
        Came and went
In between the mirrors
        By the carousel
                With capes on

Down By the River

March 7, 1973

Minutes in Time

Second by second
Minutes in time
Hour by hour
Left nothing behind

Lost in the past
And found the next day
The shape of tomorrow
Adds up the same way

Summer in season
Sun at high noon
June has a reason
For not coming too soon

1984

The Thief

Have you ever been lonely
When your friends have forgot
Like cuts never healing
Or a thief never caught

These things that are stolen
From under your bed
The bread and the butter
The thief is now fed

The circle the cycle
The wheel that spins round
Soon lands on your number
Then slips out of town

We live under cover
Sleep through the day
The moon for a partner
Champagne everyday

1980

Pictures in Life

Jungle bed dreamers
City street prayers
Flying on rainbows
Running down stairs

Puppy dog horseshoes
Eating dry ice
Kitty cat slippers
Bear traps for mice

Smokey ghost towers
Islands in sight
Waves on the water
Pictures in life

Sunny cotton candy
Rainbow gumdrops
Shooting star sunrise
Tall as treetops

1982

Ode to Tom Robbins

Got my head over a cowgirl
Clicking both feet in the air
This heart of mine a wagon wheel
Rolls along a gypsy trail

It's been said that every cowboy
Has rode this dusty trail
Empty bottles and bar room songs
Too many horses sold for bail

Whoa-Ho gypsy cowgirl
Westward tracks and midnight tales
She got the blues gypsy cowgirl
Whiskey jars and county jails

Dark haired gypsy cowgirl
In the saddle eyes of blue
Claims her name is Jellybean
She's a cowboy's dream come true

Whoa-Ho gypsy cowgirl
Westward tracks and midnight tales
She got the blues gypsy cowgirl
Whiskey jars and county jails

Now Sissy and Jellybean
Are riding down that trail
Even Cowgirls Get the Blues
Leavin' me without bail

Whoa-Ho gypsy cowgirl
Westward tracks and midnight tales
She got the blues gypsy cowgirl
Whisky jars and county jails

1978

Before You Grow Old

Play with fire
Play all the games
Needs and desires
Found many ways

To reach what you want
To get to that goal
To beat all the odds
Before you grow old

Some call it soul
Some don't even know
What moves us along
Before we grow old

The clues and the meanings
We should never hide
To show ourselves and open
The doors locked behind

1981

Moonlight Reflections

Reflections at the water's edge
Relic's rays and crashing waves
Booming thoughts like pounding rain drops
On a beach of salt sandy rocks

Falling stars twinkling are
Toting weight much to fate
Crashing down drilling holes
Too big to use for cereal bowls

Flying to walk with the man on the moon
That puts us to sleep while
Visions of expeditions travel in our heads
Boiling our money to greenish death beds

1972

A Signal

A signal
A cycle
      A stop and go rhyme

A wink and
A nod
      Two peas in a pod

Like flowers
The hours
      I wait till I wilt

The showers
Devour
      Homes built on stilts

The flood
And flowers
      All washed away

The signal
Has changed
      Don't Walk
            Only Run!

Fall 1980

Fruit of Life

By and for the plight of two
That flow with a fragrance
Of lilies . . . underneath the moon

For that an award
Of fantastic fooly bears
And polygenetic corpulent fring-fells

As products drown the consumer
Buying frost flown bon-bons
With strawberry centers
In polka-dot boxes

Gawking galore gazing gone
Through throughout the gaping hole
Wondering why but receiving sighs
From the thought police
With dice in their pockets
And cards up their sleeves

Ready to confiscate your capital
Because the fruit grower's express
Is expressing all its fruit —
For the fruit of life
Is the sustenance of all

April 16, 1973

All the Kings Men

Towers of flowers
Colors in time
Sunshine and showers
The taste of fine wine

A dollar an hour — and
Feather ink pens
Meat and potatoes — and
All the king's men

Strawberry soda
Cherry gumdrops
Candy bar wrappers
The waterproof watch

Streetlights and sidewalks
Small town bus stops
Motels or hotels
Barstools — bad luck

Sharp cheddar cheese
The man in the moon
Fingers in mouse traps
Pianos in tune

Corn flakes and roses
Four Sundays a month
Monday Night Football
Three downs and then punt

Oil and gold mines
Religious gas lines
Gallons of money
The blind flying blind

1980

All Your Heroes

Well you can super-size me
Energize me or
Cut me to the bone

Take me back
With a Cracker Jack
Or buy a small cell phone

Because my computer screen
Is like a laser beam
A cyber happy home

Just one request
That time will test
Where the deer and the antelope roam

So to all my friends and neighbors
And doctors on TV
I sing to you a simple song
Of future history

Hold on to all those heroes
We all know who they are
Hold on to all your heroes
They live so close not far

Well I've never had a Mac Attack
Or a heart attack
But I've seen the light of day

It shines on through
The ozone layer
As the sunscreen melts away

Because I know that Jesus
Loves me every day
And Hollywood and Robin Hood
Will save the American way

Hold on to all those heroes
We all know who they are
Hold on to all your heroes
They live so close not far

Fall 2004

Is There Anybody Out There

Is there anybody out there
Is there anyone around
I'm-a gonna shout now
So long I'm going home

Is there anybody listening
Is there anybody here
I'm-a gonna tell you
Shout it in your ear

Turn on your radio
Turn the record loud
Let the music play
Get Off-a My Cloud

Message on your cell phone
Text message on your screen
Commercial on the TV
Picture magazine

Lies in all the headlines
Enough to make you scream
Is there anybody out there
Is there anyone around

I'm-a gonna shout now
So long I'm going home
Is there anybody listening
Is there anyone around

I'm-a gonna tell you
Shout it in your ear
Turn on your radio
Turn the record loud

Let the music play
Get Off-a My Cloud

2007

FAITH & FAMILY

Art transcends all and holds us together

Church

Did you ever sit and wonder
Of where you're going to go
And that if you didn't sit on Sunday
To Heaven you surely would not go

Praise the Trinity the pastor would proclaim
As he would preach the hour away
The devil's dead so reject hate
Then temple hands and pray

Don't test your fate
Heal and bend to faith
Never hesitate for goodness sake
To go and sit each Sabbath day

And we'd sing the hour away

Onward Christian Soldiers!
Marching As To War!

Oct. 1971

A Wind's Mellow Song

Let the sun warm your soul
Let the willows shade your head
Admit God into your heart
And He shall shelter your bed

Lure your thoughts like cool mellow winds
Waving the colors and petals within
Creativity is the ability to see and respond
So create a new wind's mellow song

Billow like clouds off some wise man's pipe
And you will captivate thoughts white
For clean is white and white is clean
Be snow white bright with everlasting clean

March 1973

Give God a Chance

The ever powering God
Of smokestacks and strong backs
Brings the man a check
To be spent
Not lent
On the Almighty God

Give the church a chance
Carry no lance
It provides
To all tides
Of white, and black, red too

For me and you
Everlasting joy
Will knock at your door
Bringing love, not selling commodities
Live and be loved by God

February 1973

To Her Savior She Sings

Out near Lawyer's Canyon
Where the cottonwoods grow
Chief Joseph helped the white man
By the Clearwater flow

Prairie town dry land
Grandma's six sons
She raised just one daughter
Her life brought sixty young ones

Some called her an angel
Without any wings
All called her a saint
To her savior she sings

To her savior she sings
To her savior she sings
Some called her an angel
Without any wings

Eternity served daily
On homemade plates
A slice of Americana
It's all good — have a taste

Candies and cookies
Hands of caring silk
Fresh bread in the oven
Needles and quilts

Out near Lawyer's Canyon
Where the cottonwoods grow
Chief Joseph helped the white man
By the Clearwater flow

To her savior she sings
To her savior she sings
Some called her an angel
Without any wings

2010

That Train

That train is leavin' now
Headed homeward bound
Headed for the sunshine
Leavin' this here town

Have your ticket ready
The conductor's checking all
He rides the rails every day
"All Aboard" his lonely call

The engineer is steady
He works his engine right
Keeps that train on time
Drivin' down the line

That train
That train
Leavin' here today

That train
That train
Takin' me away

That train is gonna find you
Lost one lonely night
Find you when you're dreamin'
That train will make things right

I heard that lonesome sound
Come calling out for me
Telling me it's time to go
Ride that train to God's Glory

That train is heaven bound
Headed for those Pearly Gates
Bound for Glory on the highest
Freedom is now found

That train is gonna find you
Lost one lonely night
Find you when you're dreamin'
That train will make you right

2006

Waddell Street

Say a prayer on Waddell Street
At the brick house down the lane
Home to many children
Birthplace of our name

And think of those before us
That rode the eastern plain
And them with Robert the Bruce
Who fought for freedom's gain

So when you leave, head to the bar
On Carrickcarden Lane
And toast to all, including me
Plus, John and George and James

2008
Haiku for Cousin MC
at Glasgow, Scotland Family Home

I Saw Jesus

I saw Jesus yesterday
But then he turned away
Carrying the Bible
Without a word to say

I saw Jesus on the river
Stepping stone to stone
Couldn't walk on water
Chilled me to the bone

I saw Jesus at a bus stop
A rain storm just arrived
He was waitin' on a Greyhound
For a front seat Heavenly ride

I saw Jesus on a back street
Where homeless people hang
They looked so very helpless
Jesus looked the same

I saw Jesus yesterday
But then he turned away
Carrying the Bible
Without a word to say

I saw Jesus on the highway
At a ten car accident
Hitchhiking off in silence
Right past the ambulance

I saw Jesus watching TV
Fundamental station on demand
Seven hundred channels
Remote control in hand

He tuned in every channel
Watched the War on HD TV
Then switched to Sunday Football
And asked for Dos Equis

Then I saw Jesus on the river
Stepping over every stone
Walking on the water
Bringing me back home

2007

Bootleg Mountain

Up on Bootleg Mountain
We don't drink no beer
Up on Bootleg Mountain
Been my home for years

Give me moonshine whiskey
When my throat's bone dry
Give me greenback dollars
And give my 'shine a try

Daddy was a bootlegger
Six bottles every day
And when he up and died last year
We laid his soul away

Back in yonder hollow
Is where Daddy spends his days
I go visit every Sunday
Place a bottle on his grave

Now it's me and this here still
Up on a mountain top
Daddy's liquor in my veins
Don't think I'll ever stop

And when I do
Guess I'll find the Lord
But first a bottle — and then religion
The lightning — then the sword

2008

Skyler & Cass

Skyler and Cass
One lad and one lass
Stars both of you
Your light it does cast

Upon me so proud
Beside me at last
You know how I love you
With a heart beating fast

Grow strong and be brave
Each day is a gift
Be free and live long
Your legacy shall last

And when you grow old
Stay young every day
Live life each dawn
Like it's your last

Love you like mountains
Love you like rain
Love you forever
Love always remains

2007

THE NATURAL WORLD

Poetry and art bring to the human race
what nature cannot complete

When Stars Were Road Signs

A world without man
Of space before time
The beginning of life
When stars were road signs

Take a country mile
Hold it in your hand
It brings a certain smile
One to share and lend

Mother Nature's a wise one
She knows her children well
Fields of sons and daughters
Preserve and balance this land

1979

The River Grande Ronde

Come sit with me darling
On the banks
Of the River Grande Ronde

Near the willow
Where we once
Stood strong

Bring me flowers
Each day
In the springtime

In the fall
Bring a blanket
Of leaves

And when it's
Too cold in winter
Please darling just
Sing this song to me

On the banks
Of the river
Grande Ronde

Where wishes come true
One for me
Two for you

I wish we were
Still holding hands
Walking along

On the banks
Of the river
Grande Ronde

2007

Word River

Flowing water over words
Sounds beneath a mountain sky

Every rock a granite choice
River blanket fluid voice

Every day the river swirls
Above each sentence water curls

Timeless ticking liquid clock
Every rock a river tock

Endless river ticking time
Water words making rhyme

Springtime river talks and moves
Speaking words a rock that soothes

Flowing water nouns and verbs
Speaking from a river word

Fluid water creased and swirled
Every pebble a letter learned

Listen for the lost language
Talk to me — word river world

April 1979

On The Shore

Wait for me dear
On the shore
Of the river

Till I gather
Some feathers
To build me a wing

And fly back to you
Once the weather
Hits spring

On the shore
Of the river
Love brings

When the leaves
On the trees
Sprout again

And our love
Like a Bird Song
Will sing

On the shore
At the side of
The river in spring

Wait for me dear
Together we'll be
Like two love birds alone
Singing our song

On the shore
Of the river
We'll be

May 1, 1980

Grande Ronde

Some talk of big water in springtime
When the current can outrun a deer
Where the water runs deep as a gold mine
And they call it the River Grande Ronde

It once fed an Indian Nation
The Umatilla Warriors were strong
Now the tears of an Indian Nation
Flow in the River Grande Ronde

Some talk of an Indian Maiden
Her spirit it sings in the trees
Some say that she drowned for a loved one
I say that she drowned there for me

So bury me please by the river
Where my loved one drowned just for me
Water the flowers each day there beside us
Fresh from the River Grande Ronde

2007

There's a Buddha in The River

Buddha in the river
Mother Earth and Karma Son
Miracle of wonders
Folded into one

Wrinkled creases flowing
Water sky supreme
Dharma wheel spinning round
Tantric cycle has begun

Spirit in the water
Rise to meet the Sanskrit Sun
Drown us in Quicksilver
Zen of liquid love

River has no end
Nowhere to begin
Moon and stars divide the day
Buddha moves as one

Find balance in the river
Touchstone path from shore
Living like the ancients
Simplistic daily chore

Great Buddha in the water
Show your way to me
Noble steps of wisdom
The gilded path of love

Abandon all possessions
Choose the middle way
Turn out the Demon Devil
Give it all away

Buddha in the river
Smiling back at me
Live and die together
Yin and Yang are one

Elastic fantastic Buddha
Stretching to the sea
Drop of rain and surface spring
Come Together — flow as one

River springs from Mother Earth
Buddha shows the way
Neither one has no end
New beginning everyday

Eccentric concentric river
Circle back around
Drench me — Drown me — Astound me
Yin and Yang are one

Buddha is the river
Mother Earth and Lotus Son
Dharma Wheel absolute
We are all as one

Karma in the river
Moon and Stars and Sun
Miracle of wonders
We are all as one

There's a Buddha in the river
Smiling back at me
Teach me how to find him
Teach me how to see

1979

CHILDHOOD

Art is like freezing a youthful moment
and never letting it thaw

The Old Ball Field

The smell of dirt and a leather glove
Summer sun in the sky above
On a field of rocks and full of weeds
This was where we lived to dream

Down the block was our ball field
Second base was there to steal
Centerfield stood straight away
 Hit and run the game to play

Every day we'd gather round
Choose up teams on sacred ground
The ball on wood a homerun sound
Life was good in our small town

Never seemed to make full count
Everyone would scream and shout
A place where no one did strike out
Lessons we can't live without

The pitcher's mound was fastball trouble
Fly ball and a stand-up double
Grounders roll on dry grass stubble
Our mouth's chock-full of double bubble

2005

The Children

Don't you know that the hills are green
And the children smile
With a dream as long
As a country mile

In a world grown cold
Still the children smile
Throwing all their hopes
On a growing pile

The eyes of youth
You know they speak the truth
They believe in love
Holding hearts above

We all get a chance
To dance and sing
Some on a prayer
Some on a wing

The chance of a lifetime
I've heard the refrain
A great opportunity
A runaway train

No second chance
I've heard it before
There's no second chance
Or happy returns at the five n' dime store

Spring 1973

Graduation Day

Never cared too much for school
Always lived by the golden rule
Daddy said I'd never go too far
But mama didn't raise no shootin' star

Grandpa had a nickel for my thoughts
His coins and stories meant a lot
Grandma loved to sit and rock
Those times I've not forgot

Each spring the water filled the creek
In grandpa's yard we'd play each week
Until one day when his soul did fly
Mama said he found a greater place on high

Freedom is that graduation day
Free to live and fly away
We all go to our chosen ground
Above, beyond — freedom is now found

1976

Bring Me Back

Looking through the photos
Pushing past the years
All the different stages
Remembering those so near

Childhood days past twilight
The dates and places clear
Images of black and white
In neighborhoods held dear

Sing to me the story
Sing to me the time
When a sleepy town discovers
There's no more nursery rhyme

Why would we ever think
Anything would change
Everything was perfect
Nothing to be feared

Friends became a family
To each a brother son
Together and forever
Until we cannot run

Sing to me the story
Sing to me the time
When a sleepy town discovers
There's no more nursery rhyme

Bring me back the river
Bring me back the wine
Sing to me the story
Sing to me the time

Bring me back the river
Bring me back the wine
Sing to me the story
Sing till suppertime

Fall 2004

WAR & POLITICS

The world of creativity is a shelter from
the hard realities of life

Two-Hundred Years of U.S.A.

Two-Hundred years of U.S.A.
Home of the free and land of the brave
With Watergate and roller skates
And spacious waves of grain

Our land of milk and honey
Once held the Red Man's name
Now comic strips like politics
Are life the American way

This land without speed limit
Though we sing in harmony
Some sing of the second coming
Others dig Let It Be

From Plymouth Rock to Barrow
From sea to shining sea
The dream of every Yank is still
A paycheck on Friday

1976

Summer 1863

Running through the hills
Hiding on a mountain top
Running back down
To the valley far below

Getting low on water
Nothing to be found
But Robert E. Lee is gonna try
To put you in the ground

Riding tired horses
Through the Mississippi mud
From all of Grant's blue coats
In the Summer '63

Watching our backs
Thinking 'bout our darlin' ones
Heading for the Promised Land
Up in the sky above

The Old Grey Fox
And the Union Calvary
Gettysburg and Vicksburg
In the Summer '63

In the heart of Dixie
Grant was back again
With Vicksburg in his sights
Right around the bend

Gunboats were a comin'
Fighting on a moonless night
Moving all the Union Boys
Charging from the southern flank

In the second year of fighting
Vicksburg fell to Union hands
The Pemberton's fought
With the pride of Dixieland

Vicksburg ground covered in blood
The town fell to its knees
Big river red after the flood
In the Summer '63

Watching our backs
Thinking 'bout our darlin' ones
Headed for the Promised Land
Up in the sky above

The Old Grey Fox
And the Union Calvary
Gettysburg and Vicksburg
In the Summer '63

The Old Grey Fox
Headed into Gettysburg
Lookin' for a fight
Deep in Lincoln's Land

Pickett made his charge
On a bloody July 3
Shells from Little Round Top
Back to the Devil's Den

The Grey coats fell upon a ridge
They call Cemetery
50,000 dead and wounded
At Gettysburg those days

Sherman leads his war machine
Caisson's roll along
Creeks are filled with rebel red
In the Summer '63

Watching our backs
Thinking 'bout our darlin' ones
Headed for the Promised Land
Up in the sky above

The Old Grey Fox
And the Union Calvary
Gettysburg and Vicksburg
In the Summer '63

2006

Molly's Lament

Bill Henry went a courting
Young Miss Molly Jean
Heart beating faster
Than a Gatling machine

First time that he saw her
At the top of the stairs
A hand me down necklace
And long yellow hair

Got married right away
Had a baby child
Then Sumter happened
And the fire spread wild

Couldn't pay no substitute
He never had a Sunday suit
Just a fruit tree picker
With a bit of 'shine in his boot

Bill Henry he got called
To the Civil War
Shipped out east
Where blood stains soil

Never set foot on Dixie ground
Never sought solace in the brigade sound
First day out Bill Henry went down
Shot by a ghost in a southern town

Now he's back home
Wheelchair bound
Can't walk can't talk can't even stare
At the man in charge who put him there

Molly Jean cries every night
Prayin' for the Lord to make it right
Waitin' for a sign to tell her why
He was in that fire fight

Out in the distance
A haunting sound
War Wagon Wheels
In the background

2006

Last Time

As the sins of the Great White Fathers are fed
I stare at my country in dread
Telling myself their statements are lies
While bitter tears drown my eyes

"Peace is at hand" says the man about Vietnam
Yet the soldier still stands
"All we need is a little more time"
But hasn't ten long years been fine

Sitting in my chair abiding grief
I pray the battle does cease
The leaves on the trees turn color
As the coat on the soldier turns red

While the leader retreats to his warm bed

Dec. 1972

Riot

Expanding tides of ill-humored jingoists
Pulsating police with clubs over heads
Devouring claws of government guards
Peaceful protesters endure lethal blows

What is gained . . . Regime Superiority
        What is lost, freedoms; we're all
                Controlled by government

Placards pertaining to tranquility
        Guns pertaining to hostility
                Voices without echoes
                      Bricks tossed

A pistol sounds
        A soul is drowned
                A Mother cries
                      The leader sees it not

Our country gone astray

Feb. 28, 1972

The American Homemade Blues

Destination Basra
And all points in between
The south lawn of the White House
And the City of New Orleans

Heck of a job there Brownie
Way to go Cheney Boy
Destination flat broke
Life the American way

There's nothing quite like
The American homemade blues
From Boston to the Bay

There's nothing quite like
The American homemade blues
It's life the American way

Destination desert ghost
Battle of blood and oil
Four bucks for a gallon
No jobs left to toil

Suppression at the voting booth
Recession everyday
Impression none for George W
Depression on the way —

Because the American Homemade Blues
Are here to stay

2007

Definite Man

We need a little patience
But the Definite Man says no
Definite Man a dirty player
Driving down a bloody road

Too many cards on the table
Too many deals gone bad
Definite Man sees nothing
Definite hands hold none

Well he's a Definite Man
With a Definite plan
Helping the aristocracy
Cause he's a Definite Man undone

The Definite Man must leave now
The best thing he could do
High water stains a neighborhood
Covers the yard where a child once stood

2005

There's No Water Left

There's no water left
In the River Mississippi
It's filled with the tears
Of Bourbon Street souls

It runs dark and long
From the heartland to the Delta
It runs with the sound
Of the last paddle-wheel

There's no water left
In the River Mississippi
It carries the homes
That the levee once held

There's no water left
In the River Mississippi
It flows with love lost
And too many headstones

Delta Queen carry me
Back to New Orleans
When the river brought dreams
Instead of the tide

Delta Queen take me
Back to New Orleans
Riverboat carry me
To the city I love

But there's no water left
In the River Mississippi
There's no wave to bring me
To that far away shore

There's no water left
In the River Mississippi
It's filled with the tears
Of Bourbon Street souls

2006

Private Bonespurs

Hide with your tribe
Play golf the next day
Fritter each hour
And Twitter away

You cheat and you lie
Fake news election
Take no responsibility
For what you have done

You call the sky yellow
Call the sun red or blue
But there's a wave that's a comin'
Gonna wash over you

Point fingers at others
For crimes you have done
Never sit in a pew
But call yourself chosen one

We're all sick and tired
Of you and your sins
General Billy Barr and the hookers
You paid off everyone

Lawless corruption — power abuse
Cover-up collusion and Moscow Mitch
Slapdash gerrymandering
Mueller proved — yer' the Witch

Hypocrite definition
Laws mean not a thing
Our Constitution for wallpaper
You've committed every sin

The fruit of Impeachment
Tastes good in the soul
Today's party of Lincoln
Has disgraced noble goals

Indictment and prison
For Individual 1
Orange jump suit new hair-doo
Justice someday will come

Dec. 2019

Bonespurs & Wiz Bang

Private Bonespurs & General Billy Wiz Bang
Are hard at work each day
Lying to the common folk
While the Bourgeoisie all play

Call it what you want to
Call it as you can
It's called un-in-factual
When Bonespurs has a plan

Call it exploitation
Call it what you may
It's blatant rigged corruption
When The Private has his way

Call Bonespurs to the rescue
Have him and Penzy save the day
Call Bonespurs to the Covid rescue
Him and Penzy —
Hope you have a real nice day

No legislation for the people
Just insults and nicknames
Children locked in cages
Where's the good in what you've done

Senate fighting for the freedom
Of Bonespur's rich cronies
And we're wearing masks and gloves
On our way to buy groceries

We're taxed more than the lives
Of Spur's elite wealthy
And we're tired of all the lies
And The Private's got plenty

Call Bonespurs to the rescue
Have him and Wiz Bang save the day
Call Bonespurs to the Covid rescue
Him and General Billy Wiz Bang —
Hope you have a real nice day

2020

George Floyd

8 minutes and 46 seconds
To burn the Good Book
8 minutes and 46 seconds
And the World shook
8 minutes and 46 seconds
A knee on his neck — his life was took
I'll never forget you George Floyd

8 minutes and 46 seconds
The time passed unheeded
8 minutes and 46 seconds
George said and he pleaded
"I can't breathe," he repeated
I'll never forget you George Floyd

Now the Country is reeling
Tear down these racial walls
That's what is needed
Black Lives Matter needs repeating
Bridges between need completed
We yearn for a compassionate leader
We'll never forget you George Floyd

Rest in Power

June 1, 2020

Here in America

I sit here in America
And argue how much time
It took the Great White Father
To threaten all mankind

I stand here in America
I howl, I bark, I scream
At all the built out places
 Where once a young man dreamed

I can't wait here in America
To rage upon the moon
Then call to all the children
With little left to choose

I snap, I snarl, I scream at America
Today not fair or just
I bark, I bite, I want America
A new America or bust

I walk here in America
Past houses, farms and fields
Land of the free and brave
Taken away from us

I run here in America
In the shoes of every foot
One step, each stride, each town
 In every neighborhood

I move here in America
On roads of cement dust
The path once just a trail
For the Red Man before us

I howl, I growl, I scream at America
Today not fair or just
I bark, I bite and want America
A better America or Bust

I reside here in America
In a home under stars above
I live and work — underpaid
In line we push and shove

I exist here in America
I pay and pay some more
Then pay to play the game
And wonder why I'm sore

I inhale here in America
I cough, I spit, I wheeze
The Aqua Lung is gone now
Too late to say yes please

We need here in America
Clean water, air and trees
Remember when you couldn't see
The air that we all need

I live here in America
I eat, I drink, I sneeze
I guess the Great White Father
Doesn't care I'm on my knees

I see here in America
All the Covid war headlines
While the undertaker works
Hours of overtime

I reject here in America
Fake News on Trump TV
All trash and dirty laundry
While "We the people" are hung to dry

I try here in America
To abide from sea to shining sea
And pray for all the souls
Lost so needlessly

I mourn George Floyd in America
Ahmaud Arbery today and yesterday
Slain by brutal crimes injustice
"Enough is enough" I say

I howl, I bark, I scream at America
A land not fair or just
I bite, I scowl, I cry, I yell
"I can't breathe" ENOUGH!

I see here in America
I watch, I wait, I hope
To see the Second Coming
Change the wrongs to right

I sit here in America
And argue how much time
It took the Great White Father
To threaten all mankind

I stand here in America
I howl, I bark, I scream
At all the empty spaces
Where once a young girl dreamed

I howl. I bark, I scream at America
Today not fair or just
I bark, I bite but thank America
Together America or bust

I rant, I rave, I love America
The only home for me
Built on grand designs
But things must change

To remain the land of the free
"We Are Stronger Together" ENOUGH!

2006/2020

NORTH FORK

The extreme grants the ability
to both lose and find one's self at the same time

Big Water

Our life is a mountain
Keeps us slowed down
Stony river by us
We live on high ground

This river a circle
Many more unfound
Its course a cycle
Our planet spins round

Big water in our valley
Flows swift between shores
Its music brings mercy
Flowing water song

Man's time booked in pages
Of knowledge on high
Each wisdom remains different
Throughout all mankind

Big water in our valley
Flows swift between shores
Today's sunrise a secret
Of a mountain life in store

May 1978

Winter's Hand

Ah! Those shortened days
When cabin fever hits
Hatchet kindling ways
Feeding the fire never quits

A difference of life-styles
Divides our lives now
With candles for light
We walk the same miles

Silent white pillars
Drift into mounds
Such beauty so harsh
Winter's hand abounds

A world carved of wood

Holds motion — Be Here Now

February 1979

The Other Side

Somebody said
Bobby MacFarland
Was living on a wire

Somebody told me
He tried to
Catch a Fire

Bobby got caught
Running with
A white tide

Bobby got caught
Across the river
On the other side

Oh Bobby MacFarland
Where did ye go
Oh Bobby MacFarland
With a head full of snow

Danced with the devil
Each step took in stride
Got caught 'cross the river
On the other side

1983

Hey Now Bobby

Hey now Bobby
What's the matter here
Hey now Bobby
What's the matter here

You and your Mistress
Ya' come around
You and that Lady
In her white gown

She didn't have to treat you
Like she did
She didn't have to burn you
But she did

She took you down the river
Down to, trouble town
She took you to the dealer
An' made you, double down

The Mistress went and used you
An' then she threw you out
The Mistress and her Voodoo
Made you scream and shout

Hey now Bobby
Look who's cryin' now
Hey now Bobby
Look who's cryin' now

1981

Logger's Dream

The logger's dream in hoot owl season
A one log load — no rhyme 'nor reason
Two bits flush and a flume log ride
Biscuits-n-gravy and flapjack wide

Hike the trail nosebag in hand
Crosscut saw for an old growth stand
Springboard notch cut with pride
Undercut the uphill side

Color green and yellow cedar
Pull the whip in frenzied fever
Kerosene to grease the saw
Tales of woe fall from his jaw

Top the spar and rig the line
High lead block for haul back time
Feed the boiler an' jam the lever
Hiss of donkey and choker chaser

The punk he whistles to go ahead slow
Widow maker spoils the show
Cribbing stacked the Shay it pulls
Dem logs to mill and steel grapple

In corks and spenders he hunts the snipe
The brush ape whittles a corncob pipe
Bull cook bean hole beaver bait
The flunky jerks on a nailed down plate

Draw a bead on side-hill salmon
Poach black tail then wedge and hammer
Smoke a pipe and sleep on hay
Work till supper and make payday

The logger's dream
On a par buckle night
A jar of 'shine — some snoose — and
Stay out of the bight!

2016

The Raven

The Raven flies
Over North Fork skies
Above all of those
Down here below

Her solace is the sky
Freedom on a breeze
Rarely touching down to earth
Doing as she please

Over spotted hills of snow
The Raven flies at will
Only taking time to stop
For her evening meal

Soaring through the clouds
Riding on the wind
Sunset sends her homeward bound
Yet tomorrow flies again

I wait to see the Raven
Her feathers black sunshine
I wait to hold the Raven
And the time when she will find

This quiet bird of one
In need of lofty wing
Carry me home - once again
For the Raven - I shall sing

First to find my wings
Then to take the flight
The Raven for a teacher
Teaching wrong from right

Life outside the nest
A leap of faith - the test
Wings on wind - soaring now
High above the rest

1980

Down in Coca Town

Coca Town is where I go
When I need to get away
Lay my head down on a cloud
Let me sing my blues away

Coca Town is where I go
When I need some sugar sweet
Fill my belly feed my brain
No friend like that big white train

Think I'll go on down the river
Maybe have an early dinner
Spill some drinks — tell some lies
Blow until the coca's dry

Head downstream and fall right down
Right smack dab in Coca Town
Pick me up and buy a beer
Argue with the Devil then spit in his ear

Make amends — buy a round
Play some cards and double down
Gamble with the Devil — bet every crown
Then lose every dollar in Coca Town

Ya' just can't bargain with the Devil
Might as well grab a shovel
Dig yourself a hole so deep
End up in big coca trouble

Knee deep in the coca
How it sparkled and it shined
Make an Old Man bulletproof
And a Young Man crawl a mile
Down to Coca Town

1978

Tell Me Bobby

Tell me Bobby
Tell me yes
Did you leave with her
Get her new address

Tell me Bobby
Tell me now
Tell me right
Cause I want to know

Tell me if
You loved her so

Tell me Bobby
Tell me yes
What did that Mistress hide
Behind her flowing dress

Was it wine and wisdom
Or was it left unsaid
Did she really break your heart
Or blow your mind instead

Tell me Bobby
Tell me twice
Was it sugar
Or was it spice

Tell me Bobby
What made that Mistress nice

Did she love you
Why did she go
You knew you loved her so
Couldn't let her go

Why did she leave you
Why did she have to go
That Wicked Mistress up and left this town
Now you're all alone

Tell me Bobby
Tell us all
About the time
You took that fall

Tell us why
You had to crawl

Tell us Bobby
Tell us why
How come that Mistress
Made you sigh

Did she tell a lie
Oh Bobby do confess

1983

River Between Us

River between us
No longer dry
Storm gone before
Seasons fly by

I know in my heart
You are the one
Deep in my soul
Lost and so blind

So many years
So many times
Red and white wine
Your smile so sublime

Cable car rides
Floods in the fall
Cutting cord wood
Climbing the walls

High on a mountain
It's easy to fall
In love with a lady
But when will she call
Lonely land between us
Too many miles to crawl

Jan. 1982

River Complete

There's a Buddha
In the river
Looking back at me

There's a spirit
In the water
Talking back to me

Let the water
Take my mind
Take it for a ride

Take it for
A long, long time
Let it make me shine

The river spins
A Dharma Wheel
Brings me back to Zen
Liquid dream never change
Yin and Yang are one

Buddha in the river
Coming back to me
Spinning cycle polish stone
Circle round the sun

Miracle of wonders
Mother Earth and Karma Child
Buddha sings a river song
Folding into one

River both of Yin and Yang
The Dharma Wheel begun
Mother Earth and Smiling Sun
Bring us back to one

Miracle of wonders
Quicksilver dream
Find your heart inside the water
Free your mind and float upstream

Get lost inside the river
Let it take you down
Bring you up — float you high
Never hit the ground

The spirit in the river
Buddha heart and smiling son
Miracle of wonders
River bring us back to one

The river roams
Over agates and stones
And sleeps in a bed
Of old granite bones

It rolls past the dreams
Every hope in-between
It runs down each valley
To the salt and sea breeze

The river will never forget
And never regret
The river the stream
A Quicksilver gleam

Stillwater hush
Moves faster to touch
Shimmer and shine
The river's all mine

The Osprey commands
The sky and the sand
Wing on the wind
Nowhere to land

The heart of the river
A rush in the air
Motion of time
Lotion of Zen

The river runs tomorrow
River has no end
Nothing left to borrow
Nothing more to lend

Buddha in the river
Smiling back at me
Live and die together
Yin and Yang are one

Find your heart inside the river
Free your mind and float upstream
Search your soul in crystal water
Discover we are one

Taste the crystal water
Drink from Dharma glass
Take in the flowing silver
Pray to make it last

Elastic fantastic Buddha
Stretching to the sea
Drop of rain and surface spring
Come Together — flow as one

Buddha in the river
Talking just to me
Spirit in the water
Teaching all to see

Buddha in the water
Looking right at me
Smiling face with shinning eyes
Yin and Yang are one

Buddha in the river
Mother Earth and Karma Son
Dharma Wheel spinning now
The cycle has begun

Miracle of wonders
Mother Earth and Karma Child
Dharma wheel spinning round
Quicksilver dream runs wild

There's a Buddha in the river
Water smiling back at me
Tells me how to find him
Teaches me to see

Great Buddha in the water
Show your way to me
Noble steps of wisdom
The gilded path of love

There's a Buddha in the river
Mother Earth is spinning round
See the Buddha in the river
Makes me wanna jump right in an' drown

The river runs tomorrow
Running right on time
Liquid gift not borrowed
Fluid words in rhyme

Buddha in the river
Mother Earth and Karma Sun
Miracle of wonders
Folded into one

Find the Buddha in the river
Smiling back at you
Buddha springs from Mother Earth
River shows the way

Elastic fantastic Buddha
Stretching to the sea
Drop of rain and surface spring
Come Together — Zen supreme

The Buddha is the river
Mother Earth and Karma Son
Miracle of wonders
Yin and Yang are one

1979

The Devil Held Aces

The Devil
The Angel
And the Prodigal Son

Played cards at a table
Made for just one

The Mistress
The Fortress
How the North Fork was won

They all played for keeps
The game had begun

Life on a string
A steel string at that
Across the wide water
Wilderness land

The years rolled by
Devil made his plan
A twisted game of life
Fire melts sand

The Angel flew off
As the Prodigal looked on
Devil enraged
Consuming him and those around

Fire and rain
Winters hot flame
Came cross the river
In the Devil's last name

The cards were all dealt
All in their places
Nobody knew that
The Devil Held Aces

1984

For Phaedrus

Phaedrus was Wolf
Son of Thunder
Meaning so strong
Color white wonder

Howls in the night
To run into dawn
Love for the forest
Where only wildlife belongs

Life of some sign
Known to chosen few
Stopped in his tracks
Roadside Baring

Up Highway 2

June 23, 1978

I Shall Return

Vine of maple
Moss and sandy loam

Tree of bark
Root and fiber strong

Fir of Douglas
Branch of cedar

Graceful fern
Owl and beaver

Sky of wind
Rain all season

Alder to fell
For burning reasons

The river sings
All day long

It flows of love
Then plays a song

I miss you so
Forest green

I shall return
Scattered ashes of me

2019

LOVE & MERCY

Love and mercy are the only true means
by which one can live another's life

Love Wins

Love is a rose
It flowers and grows
Love is a thorn
Tattered and torn
Love is the river
In movement and flow
Love is the water
Drenching our souls
Love is the hours
Spent holding hands
Love is the time
At night intertwined
Love is a petal
That floats till it lands
Love is the desert
Oasis in sand
Love is the wind
Sung in a tree
Love is a bird
Caught on a breeze
Love is the battle
Fought for and won
Love is the peace
We find in the end
Love wins

2019

Let's Do and Say We Don't

I tried to steal a kiss
At the county fair
But Sally said she won't

Let's do and say we don't

High up on the Ferris wheel
I tried to squeeze her tight
But Sally said she won't

We rode the carousel that day
I offered her the golden ring
But Sally she said she won't

For her I'd walk a country mile
I'd love to see a little smile
Still Sally said she won't

Let's do and say we don't

Do you
Don't you
Can't you
Why won't you

Let's do and say we don't

1973

Just Like You (Just Like Me)

Just like you
Just like me
Just like eternity

When sparks fly free
Across the desert sky
They shine so bright
Like the love in your smile

Just like you
Just like me
Just like electricity

In a past lifetime
In a place of peace
When one single word
Made the world complete

Just like you
Just like me
Just like connectivity

When the leaves fall down
Then come back in spring
You know the river flows
With the love you bring

Just like you
Just like me
Just like eternity

Fall 1974

The Beauty in You

The beauty in you
Is caught in a
Glimmer and smile

The beauty in you
Shines in a
Shimmering tide

The beauty in you
Is a star shining
Back at you

The Beauty in you
Is a beauty
So true

One part Rainbow
One part yellow
One part blue

The Beauty in You

1975

Dreams to Trade

She loved me then till ever
Now never we shall run
For the sake of living life
Not for living said

And did the life run over
And did the fears away
And did the love eternity
And did the dance together

Dreams to trade for sunsets
Dreams to trade for sale
Dreams to hide the shadows
Dreams with the wind prevail

Once there was a beginning
Once there was a girl
Once there was a sunrise
Now our dream's for sale

Fall 1976

A Change of Way

Stars above
>Speak of your name

River words
>Lead me astray

Flying life
>Sunrise of a song

Horizon music
>The love we both had won

Urantia turns
>Through fields of wheat and clay

Our history remains
>A change of way

January 4, 1977

The Perfect Place

High on a mountain
Inside a river home
Beyond the dry lowlands
A place of our own

Living and loving
All things that surround
Our life silent singing
Of story book sounds

We walk holding hands
Through a fairy tale land
In a forest of green
On trails of white sand

To reach our own place
In time we will find
Where days are of heaven
Where water is wine

This place has no cycle
To spin round our minds
It only has comfort
No stop and go signs

1980

The Way of Life Today

Some say loves stays forever
Some see love slip away
Some keep love under cover
Others hope it shows someday

This time please with feeling
The next time please with taste
The last chance may be tomorrow
With no time left to waste

Sometimes I act the fool
And play the clown for you
This game is only fun
When you're in the mood

Somedays seem so right
Then they move and change
But time flies slow
And walks by fast

The way of life today

1980

Notes on the Wind

You bring me a gift
From stars high above
Shines silver color
The color of love

The air's full of music
From the radio sound
Some jukebox is singing
Heard the world round

Listen to love calls
That come in the night
Songs with a whisper
Like a tail on a kite

Notes on the water
Rise in the wind
Blown all directions
As darkness begins

Each note is a song
Sung in four time
The blues when you're lost
Hits hard every time

Oct. 1981

Do You Remember

Do you remember
The days we had of glory
Do you remember
How the story goes

Do you remember
The sunrise of our morning
Do you remember
The time we spent back when

I still remember
Your smile and flying spirit
I still remember
That full moon night back then

There's still a new dawn
At sunset every morning
When tomorrow
Becomes yesterday

Where the end starts
And begins a brand new lifetime
In the twilight
When night time becomes day

Do you remember
The days we had of glory
Do you remember
How the story goes

Do you remember
The sunrise of our morning
Do you remember
The time we spent back when

I still remember
Your smile and flying spirit
We were treading water
On that full moon night back then

1982

Good Night

If I had the words to say
I'd say them every day
Outside a dream of rainbows
The color of lost days

If I had the foresight
To see the coming storm
I'd turn to face the wind
And begin to be reborn

All the years of heartache
All the pain so deep
I took all that I could take
Then you stole from us in sleep

Years of time between
The ups and downs and strife
I wake up every morning
Just to say goodnight

2009

Every Day We Die a Little

Every day we die a little
Give in to all the pain
And every night you lie and quibble
Then don't clean up the stains

Take out all the trash
Sweep and clean the floor
Throw away all our dreams
Trade in all our sails

Where once a wind blew strong
And brought all of our dreams
Now the stillness of the water
Drowns out all that remains

Take and take until it's gone
With nothing left to sell
Every day we die a little
From every lie you tell

2009

I Need a Match

I called up my baby
On the telephone
Have ya' got any matches
I said all alone

I'm in need of a fire
To burn in my soul
The water is risin'
It's taken a toll

I'm needin' a match
To light up the way
I'm needin' a match
Ta' travel the highway

There's lava that's burnin'
Deep in my veins
It's burnin' me up
Not lettin' me go

There's not enough water
To drown out the flame
The flame's getting higher
No water to tame

I'm needin' a match
To light up the way
I'm needin' a match
Ta' travel the highway

So I wrote to my baby
To kindle her soul
With words to stay warm
A blanket of gold

She lives in a town
Carved out of wax
From candles long burned
By a path without tracks

I'm needin' a match
To light up the way
I'm needin' a match
Ta' travel the highway

1977

Did You See the Moon Last Night

Did you see
The moon last night
A circle not yet found

Did you see
It was incomplete
Not the perfect shape of round

But it shown so bright
A beam so right
It lit a gilded path to you

And gave us a chance
To maybe dance
Then melting into one

Did you see
The moon last night
A circle incomplete

Did you know
You make me smile
I'm no longer obsolete

Like a circle spins
Around the moon
It brings us back to one

I know you saw
The moon last night
Cause you had me at chainsaw

2016

There you are

There you are
Gypsy star
Harmony
Rhapsody
Everything
There they are
Moonlight stars
Light the way
A path we'll stay
Cheese an' wine
Starlight shine
La Crème' Fraiche
Berry vine
Amber moon
Flowers bloom
The promise of soon
Turned out true

2016

The Wood Carver's Daughter

The wood carver's daughter toils daily
While she whistles a lullaby tune
She adds to her woodpile in silence
Then smiles at the sky crescent moon

The wood carver's daughter brings color
Mostly green and the brilliance of blue
She sleeps with antiques in a meadow
Keeps a rocking chair for Solstice in June

She dreams through the night and dances
Beneath cedar limb branches she twirls
With a tambourine tap and a two finger snap
Her auburn hair flowing in curls

Dancing in warm summer moonlight
Her arms raised up high with a flair
She twirls round a fire of embers
Sleeps tight in the clear mountain air

The wood carver's daughter dreams daily
A wood splitting man does too
For the chance they can spend together
Spinning cartwheels 'neath a sky crescent moon

Like a Buddha the wood splitter thinks
The wood carver's daughter does too
Like Siddhartha they wait and they fast
For spring and the promise of soon

2016

Don't Leave Your Love Behind

Daddy was a miner
Uncle John was too
Daddy he was solid
Break a rock in two

Mama danced on New Year's
With Daddy all night long
Next day Daddy had to punch the clock
Out the door and he was gone

Daddy went down the Sago
One last time to the mine
Please don't go down the Sago
Don't leave your love behind

Word spread fast 'bout the Sago
Fire, deep down in the hole
Thirteen men once just boys
Now Mama prays for Daddy's soul

Don't send me any flowers
Just send me all your love
He left us in the morning
A miner he once was

Daddy went down the Sago
One last time to the mine
Please don't go down the Sago
Don't leave your love behind

A note he left his sweetheart
"I'll see you on the other side"
Cold, cold ground now between them
Mama once was his Sunday bride

West Virginia heartache
Love left down inside the mine
Rest assured my darling sweetheart
Nothing real does ever die

Daddy went down the Sago
One last time to the mine
Please don't go down the Sago
Don't leave your love behind

Jan. 2006

THE
GREAT
BEYOND

Art and poetry are protests
against man's ultimate fate

It's All I Need to Know

It's all I need to know
That you can see me here below
It's all I need to know
That you are safe and warm

It's all I need to know
That you can still be by my side
As I walk this painful path
Along life's riverside

It's all I need to know
It's all I need to know

I can see you now
Riding on a cloud
I can hear you now
Speak without a sound

I can see you now
Smiling back at me
I can hear you now
Saying it's okay

It's all that I can do
To understand what you've gone through
It's all that I can do
To release my life from you

It's all that I can do
To keep the fire bright
It's all that I can do
To make this wrong seem right

It's all that I can do
It's all that I can do

I can see you now
Riding on a cloud
I can hear you now
Speak without a sound

2008

The Banks of the River Grande Ronde

Remember the time
When we once roamed
On the banks of the river Grande Ronde

When you told me
You loved me
Then and forever
And this place would always be home

Where our children would grow
And the seasons would show
All the colors of life then and now

And the circle of life
Would spin us around
Until we found
We'd grown old

So bury me darling
On the banks
Of the river Grande Ronde

Near the willow
Where we once
Stood strong

Bring me flowers
Each day
In the springtime

In the fall
Bring a blanket
Of leaves

And when it's
Too cold in winter
Please darling just
Sing this song to me

On the banks
Of the river
Grande Ronde

Where wishes come true
One for me
Two for you

On the banks
Of the river
Grande Ronde

2015

Done, Done, Done

It seems I'm down to my last cigar
The road I traveled it's gone too far
In the end it's all for show
Ask me why and I still don't know

Never been to Paris or Rome
Never seen past the gates of home
In the end it's all for show
Ask me how and I still don't know

Well I'm done, done, done
There's no tellin' if I've won
It never was the best again
Cause I'm done, done, done

Susie and me at the restaurant
Speakin' diatribes likes and wants
Wishin' Susie and me were back again
Telling stories down on the waterfront

Well I'm done, done, done
There's no tellin' if we won
I'll never be so young again
Cause I'm done, done, done

Take me Lord — I'm done

2016

A New Kind of Yesterday

The years roll by
And I'm still waiting for
A new kind of yesterday

The kind of life
We used to have
Before tomorrow comes

But it's too late
For second comings
And second helpings too

Cause we're all stuck
In this place where
Once there were so few

I'm thinking that
Something may pass me by
Before I slip away

Into the dreams
That lay ahead
In my future days

But there's still time
To dream about
A new kind of yesterday

That finds us here
Waiting for
One true dream today

2008

Into the Purple Valley

I can see the sunrise fading
Daybreak into dusk
I can feel the life spark wither
Turning back to dust

Wash away the winter
Bathe my soul in spring
Cleanse the vital spirit
Carry me Little Wing

Fly the coming darkness
Soar to places past
Dream in lofty vastness
Climb the trail at last

Sing to me Black Peter
Chant the words in song
Talk with me Saint Peter
As we walk along

Into the Purple Valley
On a path of blue and gold
We taste the ripe strawberry
Before the season's cold

For want of life with music
For love of mystic song
For now I must be leaving
To this earth — I say — so long

The Prince of Pinehurst has Passed

2009

Fade To Black

Fade to black
From the white
Time to draw the blinds

Time to play
Not Fade Away
Time to toe the line

We peaked too soon
Rode that wave
Hit the beach each noon

But the party's over
I'm all undone
I've seen my last full moon

Fast forward to the past
Rewind me to the day
When life was full and I was young
And then please push re-play

Fade to black
From the white
Time to fare thee well

To all my friends
We sure had fun
Back there in the day

The world was ours
A grand playground
We Rocked Around the Clock

But the time has come
To Lay Me Down
And travel the Last Highway

2009

Fly the Blue Wind

I've spent all of
My promises
I've used up
Every dream

But it's time to
Fly the Blue Wind
And leave this
World between

The other side
Of this life
And a world
We've never seen

Fly the Blue Wind
Ride the high breeze
To the Great Beyond
Hush now child — there is no reason to cry

Celebrate the life
Mourn the loss
The price that
We all must pay

So bury me darling
Under shade of green
Bury me darling
Neath the old willow tree

See to the children
See to their health
And never dear darling
Tell them the rest

Check with the Parson
Check on the guests
Lunch with the Undertaker
Then pray for the best

Don't cry for me
Not like the rest
Fly the Blue Wind
I've flown my last nest

2008

Purgatory Bus Stop

Standing at a Purgatory bus stop
Waiting at the end of the line
Don't know when my ride is comin'
Guess I've got plenty of time

Standing at a Purgatory bus stop
I'll be Heaven-bound in a while
But if that bus don't get here soon
I'll be walkin' a Purgatory mile

Maybe I'll just hitchhike to the Promised Land
Stick out my thumb and smile
I'm headin' on up to Eden
Gonna go there in high style

I'm takin' a trip to The Great Beyond
To see my old friend Reno
Gonna tell him that his loved ones
Will see him in the bye and bye

2010

COSMIC COMMENTARY

Art allows one to enter its world
from any angle then exit with a new outlook

FEAR AND LOATHING
IN THE KINGDOM OF HEAVEN

For the last fifty odd years I've felt as if Hunter S. Thompson and I shared the same strain of DNA. I loved that locked in feeling I got whenever reading his latest screed against some sort of political, judicial, social or racial wrongdoing. And now with the passing of Hunter I've lost the voice that showed me the truth, the voice of our generational soul.

Back in 1972, when I was in high school, I stumbled upon Hunter's seminal work, *Fear and Loathing in Las Vegas*, spotting it on the rack at the local bookstore downtown — with that Ralph Steadman desert scene cover pulling me in. Of course I loved reading Hunter's articles in Rolling Stone, especially the one about his running for Sheriff of Pitkin County in Colorado on the Freak Power ticket so I was aware of the man and his work. But I bought the *Vegas* book and went out on the sidewalk on California Street in Everett, sat down with my back against the building and started reading. The first line bit hard, *"We were somewhere around Barstow on the edge of the desert when the drugs began to take hold."* Wow! Did I just read that right? I'd never read or even heard of an author writing such a deliberate stigma-like passage to begin a book like that before! As I worked my way through the pages I told myself, "This is exactly what you've been looking for." And truly it was.

I was hooked. *Hell's Angels* was next. That was wild, him living with the Angels in San Francisco and then getting the crap beaten out of him at the end. After that I found *Fear and Loathing on the Campaign Trail*, which was Hunter putting his own form of Gonzo journalistic spin on the 1972 Presidential election. *The Great Shark Hunt* was next and a wonderful compilation of articles and short stories, gawd I loved all his books.

The list just went on and on for me. Always searching for everything Hunter and really buying into all of his exploits. So vivid, so true, so daunting and deep. Hunter Thompson had the heart of a lion, the verbal left hook of a fighter, and the mind of an all-seeing sage who never let any issue fly under his radar. But he's gone, his voice, that voice, as left this earth.

Hunter never got the chance to fire off a round at us the time we went looking for him and Owl Farm. We never found Dr. Thompson or his place, but if we did he very well could have pointed one of his many locked and loaded firearms in our direction. It was back in the summer of '81 when we made that inquisitive side trip. And like anyone else looking to catch a glimpse of Hunter, we ended up in the Woody Creek Tavern, too out of our comfort zone to even ask where he lived.

However, if Hunter could have been here during the turbulent and uncertain times of Trump, I know for a fact that he would have snuffed Trump's chances at ever winning the GOP nomination. I say that because during the presidential primary in April of '72 Hunter planted a phony story on Maine Senator Edwin Muskie in the press under the headline, *Big Ed Exposed as Ibogaine Addict*, about a Brazilian doctor treating Muskie with a "brain paralyzing" hallucinogenic drug. It caused Muskie to immediately slide in the primary polls and quickly took him out of the presidential race. I'm positive that Hunter would have used any tactic necessary to save the planet from Donald Trump, a feat that no prosecutor or journalist (as of this writing) has accomplished.

But since I missed counting coup on Hunter in the Woody Creek Tavern all those years ago I'm planning on meeting him someday in the Kingdom of Heaven. I want to shake his hand while thanking him for speaking truth to power and being an inspiration for my generation.

> *"I have no idea where we're going,*
> *but I think we'll get there on time.*
>
> – Reno O'Riley

On Deck with H.S.T.

I heard a voice one day
But now I'm standing in the rain
Those words of truth
Now the Hunter's been caught

The talent has left this town
A real connection gone
That clear and unquestioned heart
Beats out a story — his song

It's the experience that counts
To stomp on the terra
King hell-bent
A Gonzo on ice

The final sayonara

Gonzo the Comet
Gonzo the King
The King is Dead
Long Live the King!

Stuff explodes!

In the year of our Lord: Feb. 2005

Amen

SEND HELP...
BUFFALO BILL'S SURROUNDED!

I was driving from the airport to a music festival high in the Rockies during the summer of 2007 when I decided to pay a visit to Buffalo Bill Cody's Grave, just west of Denver off I-70. Many a time I'd zoomed by the extra-large exit sign for the site when I lived in Summit County 25 years before but this time my curiosity got the best of me, so I took the off-ramp and headed into the foothills.

It's easy to see why Buffalo Bill requested the pine studded bluffs of Lookout Mountain for his final resting place. Winding through prairie grass hillsides, Buffalo Bill's Grave sits near the edge of a cliff high above the valley floor above the Modern Day Mess called Denver. I can't hardly imagine what Bill had thought Denver would look like in 90 years, or for that matter what Cody, Wyoming, would look like, but I'm more than certain that he would have never envisioned the likes of the Front Range as it is today.

The approach to Bill's Grave was once a tumbleweed lined deer trail traveled by Native Americans. But now it's littered with modern day tipis and wickiups, all at least 3,000 square feet in size, with three car garages and equipped in every modern day appurtenance and appropriation known to man. Instead of a rutty dirt path for horseback riders and buggies, the paved road leading to Bill Cody's Grave is traveled today by 10 mile per gallon SUV's and $2,000 dollar mountain bikes.

Back in Buffalo Bill's younger days he spent nearly five years in the United States Army scouting for Indians and occasionally being surrounded by them. But now Buffalo Bill has been reduced to being surrounded by Power Lines, Urban Sprawl and Cell Phone Towers. In just 90 years after his death, Modern Man has very much so ravaged Bill's neighborhood and once pristine, uncluttered view of the Great Plains to the east.

In 1860, at 14 years of age, Willian Cody became a rider for the Pony Express and carried a Colt Dragoon and Bowie Knife for protection as he rode his route. Each rider was also provided a Bible by Wells Fargo to help them find their spiritual path on their way carrying the mail down all of those dusty trails. I can envision Bill Cody reaching for his Colt or jug of rye back then but now, I wonder if Buffalo Bill would be reaching for his Bible?

Buffalo Bill was a wealthy showman, husband, father and a true American. Much more has been said and written about this great man of the Western Frontier, but I will add this: I was saddened to see all of the modern day development that he's been surrounded by. Don't get me wrong, Bill's been rightfully honored by the dedicated lands immediately around him, but the encroachment of urban sprawl and all that comes with it, to me, was heartbreaking.

The plaque above his grave reads, "At Rest Here by His Request," and when he was laid to rest on June 3, 1917 there were but two homes located on all of Lookout Mountain. Another plaque asks for visitors to contribute to the upkeep of Buffalo Bill's Grave by tossing coins on top of his deep shaft tomb. With each quarter I flipped towards Bill Cody I couldn't help but say a prayer for him and the rest of the world.

As a veteran scout of the Indian Wars Buffalo Bill had many a skirmish against hostiles and he even claimed to have killed his first Indian as a tenderfoot at the young age of 11. So I've got to believe that if Bill had his druthers he'd very much so prefer to be surrounded by Indians, than surrounded by luxury homes and cell phone towers.

"My first plan of escape having failed, I now determined another."

– Buffalo Bill Cody

SUMMER OF LOVE

In 1967 the Summer of Love was declared by the national news media after picking up the term from The Council for the Summer of Love in San Francisco. I can vividly remember the clarion call of Grace Slick over my favorite AM radio station KJR singing, "Wouldn't You Love Somebody to Love?" Growing up in a small town north of Seattle I had no idea that an entirely different world was out there waiting to show me that I didn't have to be — just like my parents.

I'd been searching for something more in life, and knew there had to be more to life than what our parents were telling us, but I could never put my finger on what it was until one evening while watching the national news. There was Harry Reasoner on CBS doing a story on Haight Ashbury and I was literally glued to the TV screen. I thought to myself, "Look at the freedom those people have — they can do what they want and go where they want! I want that independence!" I was so tired of living in a strict Republican residence with the whole dress clothes drill of wingtips and pressed slacks every day, it just wasn't agreeing with me. Plus all of the rigid structure at home with the constant questioning of Dad's disciplinarian refrains; "When are you going to straighten up and fly right?" and, "Just what exactly are you going to do with your life?"

After that first news report of the San Francisco Hippie Culture I religiously watched the news every night for any reports on the "Scene" in California. I searched out any news items in the papers and bought every album by all the San Francisco bands that the local record store had. I loved it all right away.

I was only in the seventh grade but I suddenly discovered that I had the freedom of my own thoughts. While Dad would point and yell, "Those lazy kids are a menace to society," at the Hippies on TV, I would enjoy my own beliefs while quietly disagreeing with my Father. The personal discovery that I didn't have to think like my Father or be like my Father was truly a life transforming event and shortly thereafter I discovered a new Holy Trinity to worship: Gracie Slick, Janis Joplin, and Jimi Hendrix.

And then *Sergeant Pepper's* appeared, which for me ratified my new-minded deliberations and legitimately affirmed our generation's music. From the collage cover to the book like opening of the album itself which held the hypnotic lyrics to the songs, the Beatles had single handedly taken the reins of the Hippie Culture and validated its existence. Every free flowing song that melded into each other so perfectly from the title songs beginning to the crescendo ending of the held for ever piano chord in *A Day in the Life*, every free-thinking kid in America like me found themselves drafted into a new kind of war, a war of Flower Power and Peace and Love. Soon society was becoming dominated by teenagers and it was completely liberating. It felt like we were winning the war against the foundation of aristocracy, which to some extent had been successful in keeping a firm grip on suppressing the teenagers of previous generations.

But it really wasn't a war in the conventional sense. This was a Counter Culture War being fought by the new ideals of young people versus the puritanical, etched in stone ways of the Old World Establishment. The Summer of Love challenged the world to love and not to hate. To be free and to not confine others, and most of all to be tolerant of each other and accept, not reject the young people's points of view.

The push of the Counter Culture was similar to a War in a way; a War of Ideas and Ideals and unbelievably so it's a War that is still being fought. And isn't that a sad signpost to remind us that the world for some reason just cannot seem to evolve and love and respect each other for who we are and what we each believe in. Yes, we are all different and yes we all have different views and ideas, which is what this country was founded on, but please people, respect each other for their own separate views and don't force feed anyone your personal views and thoughts about what you may think is the right thing. Just because it's right for you that doesn't mean it's right for me. I'm talking about personal freedoms, personal liberties and personal beliefs. If you don't believe in something then just don't do it and leave it at that. Don't force me to be like you and I won't force you to be like me because I don't want to be like you and I'm sure you don't want to be like me either, thank you very much.

Some people may pose the question, "Where have you gone Summer of Love?" I say nowhere. The Summer of Love is alive and well within our own hearts and minds. Remember, this is America, a place where we can still think like we want to think, say what we want to say, be who we want to be, and do want we want to do; that is as long as we all take part in the democratic process and vote.

"Good rock-n-roll is something that makes you feel alive."

– Lester Bangs

WISHWASH COUNTY

Welcome to Wishwash County, a virtuous repose that exists by what we make of it. The address is one familiar to us all, however its whereabouts cannot be found on any map but its citizenship is growing every day. There are no chains, no holding cages, no Green Meanies and most importantly there is no negativity, only positive energy and Good Vibrations where all are welcome with love in their hearts and a devotion to The Cool Political Party in their souls.

Like a transcendental traveling side show, Wishwash County can be found anywhere that the members of The Cool Political Party find themselves. A place that knows no bounds, has no borders and welcomes all that adhere to the teachings of Martin Luther King, Gandhi, John Lennon, Bob Dylan, Paul Simon, Jerry Garcia and all peaceful and loving mantras known to mankind.

Wishwash County exists because we provide it with sustenance. We are the air it needs to breath. We are the tools it needs to get the job done. We make Wishwash County exist because we manifest it every day in everything we do and say. Wishwash County is everywhere its believers are, period.

It's where Tom Robbins lives and Richard Brautigan used to reside, where Jim Morrison is buried and Brian Wilson continues his magic. It's the melting pot of the American Dream and the root cellar for everything that's worth keeping.

Wishwash County is much alike Nutopia, the country that John Lennon and Yoko Ono created during John's unjust deportation fight. Nutopia was and still is a Conceptual Country that John devised to shelter Yoko and him and all that joined them where they taught and followed the true meaning of Peace and Love and that War Is Over, If You Want It. By forming Nutopia, John and Yoko had their own country that they and all their followers could not be deported from. John and Yoko claimed that citizenship in Nutopia could be attained by any person that declared their awareness of Nutopia. Much alike Wishwash County there are no boundaries or land in Nutopia, therefore Wishwash County can only be found in the Country of Nutopia. So join us children when we sing the praises of Wishwash County and Nutopia.

"Where Religion Ends, Philosophy Begins"

- Wanda Galore,
Spiritual Leader of Wishwash County

THE COOL POLITICAL PARTY

The Cool Political Party is pleased to announce the establishment of its Official Headquarters in Wishwash County. Founding Father of The Cool Political Party, guitar and Rock-n-Roll Hero Stephen Stills created the party as a new avenue to political thinking in 1995. Until now there has been no Grass Roots underpinnings to help support and spread the ideals of the Cool Political Party's Platform and Mantra, but the party welcomes all comers and progressive thinkers who choose to abide by the planks of the Cool Party Platform.

The platform consists of a basic mantra that comes into manifestation by each members vow to follow and uphold the beliefs of the Cool Party. All members must commit to professing and administering the Cool Party mantra each and every day while propagating the advantages of membership to all that will listen.

Wishwash County is proud to be the first county in America to be the home of the National Affairs Desk and Headquarters of the Cool Party. All members are being called upon to renew their party vows to help fill the vacuum-like void of partisan bickering, power mongering, slapdash double dealing, lying, cheating, behind closed doors lobbying, gerrymandering reversing democracy to the point where politicians are picking their voters instead of voters picking their politicians, the slashing of environmental policies and laws and the abhorrent family separation policy. The Cool Party's Platform basic thrust is to bring forward only Earth sustaining Ideals and realistic plans to save our planet and mankind.

Planks of the Cool Party Platform

1. Freedom of Speech, Freedom of Expression, Freedom to Live and to Die.
2. World Peace through negotiation over War.

3. End all Hunger. Feed the Children.
4. Affordable Health Care for All. End prescription commercials on TV to help reduce drug costs.
5. Corporate Taxation including No Tax Giveaways to billionaires. No Corporate Socialism.
6. Greater support of the Arts and Public Schools.
7. Immediate Support for Alternative Energy Sources, Green Economy Technology, Environmental Protection through Earth sustaining policies. Address Global over-Population. Recycle.
8. Tougher Gun Control Laws. End Assault Weapon Sales.
9. Complete and Total Police Reform: abolish choke holds.
10. Elimination of money and lobbying in politics. End Citizens United.
11. Immigration Reform: path to citizenship and the funding of Smart Technology Borders. End Trump's border wall.
12. One person one vote. End the Electoral College. Vote in every election.
13. Replace impeachment with new presidential removal policy and corruption laws.

These Thirteen Planks of the Cool Party are brought forward as ideals to make our world a better place; if all leaders were to follow the Mantra of the Cool Political Party every civilization and most importantly Our Planet Earth will continue, prosper, and be sustainable through time infinitum. We ask for no donations and will reject them if offered. Membership is attained simply by advocating for, adhering daily to, and supporting politicians who follow the Planks of the Cool Party Platform. Thank You for joining The Cool Political Party.

> *"With no moral compass one will
> never find the proper path to follow."*
>
> – Wanda Galore

A DAY IN THE LIFE OF THE WORLD

"Daddy, it looks like the sky is crying," I heard a young girl say to her Father as they walked out of the grocery store. Following them I looked upward and could see right away what she was talking about — long streaming light grey streaks of wispy moisture pointed straight to the ground from thousands of feet in the atmosphere. In the parking lot I noticed her tug on her Father's sleeve.

"Why are they crying?" she asked.

"Because they're sad, I guess," he replied. That same day on the east coast 33 college students were killed at Virginia Tech in a mass shooting spree that left the whole country in a comatose state. What is wrong with our world today? Why are we are killing each other while we kill the planet? What is wrong with the human condition? How long can this go on? Time to wake up America! It's time for everyone to care. Time to look around and pick up the pieces and save the planet and the human race.

Once back home all I could think about was how in the world we got to where we are now. Where did it all go wrong?

Here our planet is millions of years old, and in just a teeny tiny miniscule of that amount of time we have managed to threaten the existence of this wonderful home we call Earth. When did the downfall start? When was that exact point in time when the beginning of "The End" began?

Was it the Caveman and the wheel? The inventive Henry Ford? Or when Columbus came ashore? The Pilgrims? Lewis and Clark? No, I don't think so. Was it the almighty dollar bill? Corporate America? Religion? The Crusades? Maybe. Assault weapons? Multi-ammunition clips and magazines? Bombs? The Kennedy and MLK Assassinations? Possibly. Big Box Retail Stores and Wal-

Mart? Could be but I think not. Acid Rain? Jane Fonda? Hollywood? Stanley Kubrick's, *A Clockwork Orange*? No, a shocking movie at the time but no. Jimi Hendrix? Nope, sorry. Rush Limbaugh and Talk Radio? Dick Cheney? Closer. The Rockefellers? The Electoral College? Could be. King Kong? Mae West? Charles Manson? Rat Fink & Big Daddy Roth? The skateboard? No. The Beach Boys and surfing? Good grief no. The snowboard? No, that just ruined skiing, not the world. Yoko? No. Paul? No. Haight Ashbury? Woodstock? No. Altamont? No, that just ruined the 60's along with Manson. Malt-O-Meal? No again, that just ruined breakfast. Gasoline? Kerosene? Slot Machine? Charlie Sheen? The Prom Queen? No. No. Try again.

Was it Neutron Taco? Sorry, they only played one gig. Thunderclap Newman? Not hardly they only had one hit. Zimmerman? No way. Lennon? Nope. Joe McCarthy? Could be. Hillary Clinton? George Bush? Nancy Pelosi? Maybe for some. Or was it two occurrences that led to another larger occurrence that made "The Beginning of the End" possible? Was it Congress allowing the expiration of the Assault Weapons Ban in 2004?

Or was it the abolishment of the FCC Fairness Doctrine (est. 1949) during the Reagan presidency in 1987 that paved the way to not only create Fox News but allow it to only report what Republican pundits expound, without a required by law counterpoint view for balanced reporting, thereby driving the current occupant of the White House into the presidency and then steamrolling today's Republican Party into ignoring between 60 to 80% of the American people's concerns depending on the issue?

In my opinion, yes. I believe it was both.

> *"Politicians are like diapers,*
> *they need to be changed often,*
> *and for the same reasons."*
>
> – Mark Twain

FUNERAL FOR THE AMERICAN DREAM

Now playing on a HD TV near you, America's Funeral — there's no need to check your local listings because it's available for your viewing pleasure every day, every hour. Rest assured, all of the trusted mainstream TV channels are covering it, and the longer you watch the sooner it should occur to you that we are currently witnessing the most morally bankrupt, cheating, lying and conniving, grotesque, ill-prepared, and science-discarding Greed Head Leader of the Free World who has sullied the Presidency, debauched our sacred White House and turned the Department of Justice and the Republicans in the U.S. Senate into his own personal den of corruption. We should all be ashamed.

The Death of the American Dream was first brought to light many years ago by America's favorite Counter Culture Physician, Dr. Hunter S. Thompson. Thompson diagnosed the early symptoms of the eventual Death of the American Dream and his prognosis was correct. When the Constitution stands as merely a piece of soiled wallpaper in Donald Trump's cluttered bathroom we should all recognize Individual 1 for what he really is: a criminal douche bag bull-shitter from Queens. We have been duped, robbed, crapped on, out hustled, out hacked, and bamboozled to the 9th degree in the most heinous criminal political acts ever perpetrated against our country.

And please take note of that giant sucking sound, it's the oxygen of The American Dream exiting from the Northern Hemisphere. The vacuum-like blow hole is centered over the west wing of White House on the east coast of the United States and getting worse by the day. This vacancy of oxygen is denying the ability of the entire Trump following to think for themselves, causing them to believe that nothing else in the world matters than the current occupant of the People's House staying in power.

Enough already! Richard Nixon was an amateur compared to this guy, and why on God's good green earth would any normal thinking American place stock in a president who can barely write and doesn't take time to read? Did you know that Trump basically refuses to read because he believes the letters of the alphabet are a secret evil code his adversaries use to form coherent sentences to codify the truth and hasten his eventual political demise? Trump's pithy Twitter comments prove it!

But again, why on earth have we allowed this madman to ruin the Founding Father's framework for our country in only a few short years, while the entire GOP is silently permitting him? This just shocks the living day-lights out of me! For Criminy sakes, George W. Bush was a saint compared to this Flim Flam Man! We have been professionally skewered on the White House lawn and in our own backyards by a president that only represents billionaires, lobbyists, Putin, and polluting industries; notwithstanding the fact, in this nation under God, that Trump has not a single molecule of Divinity in him.

When we have the current Attorney General William Barr acting like a strong armed Mafia Don telling the American public that there was no collusion with Russia in the face of the Mueller Report that clearly proved beyond a shadow of a doubt 150 contacts between the Trump Campaign and Russia (confirmed by the GOP Senate Intelligence Committee) any educated thinker should deduce that Trump welcomed Russian help with open arms.

Then of course there is Ukraine and Trump's overdue Impeachment including the spineless sham Republican Senate trial without evidence or witnesses proving that Donald Trump "IS" the Deep State Witch. Oh, and don't forget Trump's idiotic ripping up of the Paris Climate Accords or, on the other hand, there's the pulling out of the Iranian Nuclear Deal which only an ill-informed chump would do. Plus there's the abandoning of the Intermediate-Range Nuclear Forces (INF) Treaty with Russia. And the insane defunding and pulling out of the World Health Organization in the middle of the Covid pandemic! Or have there been so many onslaughts by Trump and the GOP against our system of values and norms, beliefs, and the Rule of Law that it's impossible to keep track of them rendering us nauseous and exhausted?

Apparently the GOP and devoted followers of Trump do not care about what happens to the world, or our elections, their medical care and social security, or our air and water, health and safety, or economy! Are his followers pleased that the United States very well could be Donald Trump's next bankruptcy?

It's painfully obvious that Trump cannot lead or take the proper steps and make the correct decisions to protect the county from the deadly Covid-19 virus, especially with his form of reassurance denialism while at the same time attempting to revise his own verbal history and obfuscate the pandemic every single day. His ignoring at first and then downplaying of, plus his botched response to the outbreak proves he is unfit for office and raises the question of who exactly is he serving? And did he believe the Defense Production Act would automatically build PPE and Covid tests all by itself?

Trump has turned the United States into his very own Kingdom of Fear. For months, Americans were, and still are, trapped inside their homes, forced to hide in terror of the deadly virus. That's because he treated the early warning signs of it the same way he treated legally served subpoenas during his impeachment; he ignored them because Truth is his adversary. The Covid pandemic has become a monumental failure in leadership for Trump that's been documented in real time on TV. As of this writing it has killed one-hundred thirty thousand innocent people (and counting) and put over 42 million Americans out of work! I can't help but ask the question: Is America Great Again yet?

Every day when he did his panic fueling press lashings (briefings) Trump had the gall to stand in front of the cameras and self-congratulate himself repeatedly for doing a disgraceful job handling the pandemic and had toddler-like temper tantrums with reporters who posed serious valid questions. All Trump did during the Covid panic was work behind the scenes to come up with enough lies to fill the time slot of his daily echo chamber TV show. If he was truly working on the pandemic he wouldn't have had two hours to spend standing at the podium playing his never ending blame game. But then there's his factional audience.

I guess Trump must emit an electro-magnetic field of voo-doo fakery that his followers are lured to and become so mesmerized with that it negates all rational thinking. They must take comfort that Trump does their thinking for them, which is so incredibly absurd because I've never understood the "current occupant" to be any kind of deep thinker or known of him to be a follower of Christianity.

How will Trump-vangelicals talk to their grandchildren in heaven, after the earth dies? What will those Trump followers say when they are confronted with the ghosts of their legacy about why they voted for the climate and initial Covid denier? How will they explain and answer to their descendants? Will they reply with, "Well, it was going to happen anyway?" Or, "Sorry, I believed the lies." Or worse yet, "Please forgive me, I promise I'll never do it again." Good grief people!

Why is it that the GOP is so thoroughly bent on doing nothing for the majority of our citizens, the country, or the planet? It's my firm belief that all leaders should be a positive force in the world and not some contrarian figure who only runs for office to serve themselves.

There is no need in the world for people like Trump who choose to divide, deceive, push false narratives, and say not a single thing about reforms in the wake of the brutal police murders of George Floyd, Ahmaud Arbery and Breonna Taylor. The long arm of the law did finally charge the four Minneapolis policemen in the killing of George Floyd: one for 2nd degree and the other three for aiding and abetting murder.

And while the country was protesting the Floyd killing what did Trump do? Like a spoiled child he hid in the White House bunker and tweeted that he was going to unleash vicious Secret Service dogs on the protesters outside. What a scared little chicken-shit!

But instead of dogs he used tear gas and percussion grenades to remove those peaceful protesters from Lafayette Square, just so he could pose for a photo-op in front of St. John's Church, the church of Presidents, and hold up the Holy Bible; looking unsure of what it actually was or how to respectfully handle it. Then, like a failed dictator of a dystopian state Trump stood in front of the church, bellowing, "We have a great country . . . the greatest country in the world, it's coming back strong, greater than ever before."

He returned to our cherished White House, walking first past walls plastered with graffiti intended for him and then between two lines of weapon-clad soldiers in combat gear leading up the front drive while pathetically clapping his hands like he was at one of his rallies!

The Bishop of St. John's, Mariann Edgar Budde, said it best, "His officials cleared peaceful protests with tear gas and horses and walked on to the courtyard of St. John's Church and held up a Bible as if it were a prop or an extension of his military and authoritarian position, and stood in front of our building as if it were a backdrop for his agenda. I was deeply disappointed that he didn't come to church to pray, he didn't come to church to offer condolences to those who were grieving, he didn't come to commit to healing our nation — all the things that we would expect and long for from the highest leader in the land."

I would hope that most Christians would've been revolted by Trump's sacrilegic stunt at St. John's. As a God fearing citizen I truly wish that his Christian followers would see past the phony evangelic veneer that Trump attempted to put forth, and not only on just that day, because he's using the scriptures for personal gain, and not practicing them.

America, we need to either make a number of serious immediate changes to who our political leaders are or we might as well order the tombstone and put some money down on the cemetery plot for the Funeral of the American Dream. Because we are currently witnessing the composition of our own Obituary, the Crucifixion of the Constitution, and the reprehensible homicide of everything else we hold dear because the blindfold on Lady Justice has been ripped off and she does NOT like what she sees!

"Donald J. Trump is the most Dangerous Person in the World."

- Wanda Galore

LOST WEEKEND

Rolling over on my back and rubbing the sleep and hair from my eyes, the first thing I focused on was the phony blue plastic light fixture on the ceiling with its etched white stars and moon. Mom had bought the thing years before when I was in grade school and made Dad put it up for her. I was pretty young at the time but could remember him complaining about doing it, wanting to hire someone to install it and them getting into a big disagreement. I was beginning to replay the whole sequence in my mind when the phone rang, jarring me out of my momentary trance — I already knew it would be Dan Driscoll. I hopped out of bed and went down the hall to answer it.

"Hello?"

"Hey Bobby, it's Dan. Are we still gonna do that hike we talked about? The weather is supposed to be perfect all weekend!" he said, his voice bright and eager.

"Shit yeah! Reno and Jerry wanna go, spoke with 'em yesterday. I got my backpack all set up and packed last night."

"Okay. How 'bout if we meet up at Reno's at around 11:00?"

"Sounds good, I'll call 'em. See ya' in a bit," I replied, hanging up the receiver. After a quick shower I called Reno first and then Jerry Morgan, he was still up for it and almost ready. I let Mom know I was going on a hike for the weekend while I wolfed down a bowl of cereal and five minutes later Jerry pulled up in his yellow '61 Impala, honking his horn. So I walked out the front door with my backpack and over to my van to make sure it was locked then down to the sidewalk.

"You wanna drive?" I asked, knowing full well how much he loved to be behind the wheel of his car.

"Sure. Hop in!" he answered, through the open passenger side window. I tossed my pack into the backseat and we were off.

It was Labor Day weekend, our last chance to blow off a little steam before Driscoll started community college and Reno went back to high school for his senior year. As for Morgan and I, we'd both been working since graduating back in June. Jerry had a job at an auto body shop and I worked for a foundry, grinding steel. Let's just say that since we all still lived with our parents we needed to get out of town for a few days.

When we pulled up in Steve O'Riley's alley he saw us from his backyard and grinned that wry Irish grin of his. Then he brushed his long frizzy bangs from his eyes and went back to work on whatever it was he was doing. A sleeping bag, faded jean jacket, porcelain plate, and a few other items lay in a heap next to him. I guessed they were things he was bringing along.

"Mornin' Reno," I said as Jerry and I got out of the car. "Whatcha got there?"

"I thought I'd build myself a backpack," he replied, tying what looked like some kind of netting to a couple of short 2 x 2 pieces of lumber for a frame. As we got closer I could see that he had some tennis netting and quickly realized where he'd gotten the material from since he lived across the street from the city courts.

"Looks like you've got some fine park department building materials there, Reno," I joked, and then laughed and asked, "That's gonna be a backpack?"

"You bet, Bobby," he answered, standing up and lifting the finished product over his shoulders by its rope straps then trying it on. "It'll be a heck of a lot lighter than whatever you two have."

"Shit, I don't have a backpack. What kind of hike are we planning on anyway?" Jerry asked, looking back and forth at each of us just as the sound of a motorcycle boomed out through the North Everett neighborhood.

"Sounds like Driscoll's here," I remarked. We all turned our heads to see Dan Driscoll turning into the alley on his raked 650 Triumph chopper, all flashing chrome and roaring thunder. He had on a red down coat, blue jeans, hiking boots and his signature white motorcycle helmet with black visor. A giant green rucksack was tied behind him to the polished steel second-rider back rest, an extra helmet was hanging from it. As he rolled up he pushed out the kickstand with a boot heel, came to a stop and shut down the motor.

"How we doing?" he asked, smiling like he'd just been paid. Dan took his helmet off and a wild kinky jangle of black hair ballooned outward from his head like each strand was a spring. Driscoll glanced over at O'Riley's homemade backpack, a quizzical look came over his face.

"We're good," I replied, but Dan craned his neck while trying to keep his eyes glued to the 2 x 2's and netting hanging on Reno's back.

"What on earth is that?" he asked, grinning as he walked behind him, grabbing the flimsy contraption and tugging at it a little.

"Oh, this?" Reno replied, taking it off and then holding it up. "I'm proud to say that it's a poor man's backpack. And, it's collapsible," he said, holding and moving it in his hands like an accordion. We all laughed heartily.

"And what's with that thing you've got? Christ, it looks big enough to hold everything in yer' mom's fridge!" Reno cracked, pointing at Driscoll's rucksack.

"I wish it was stuffed with grub," he answered, motioning towards his pack. "Got my sleeping bag and a string hammock in it, along with a cook pot and a few other items."

"What?! No food?" Reno quipped. "What about you guys? You bring anything to eat?" Jerry and I shook our heads.

"I guess we'd better make a run to the B & M," Steve suggested.

"And we're gonna need plenty of beer," Morgan added.

"I've got just the place," Driscoll quickly offered. "The little old lady that has the market over on 19th! She's been selling to me lately so we should go there first. Only six bucks for a case of Lucky."

"Well let's get goin' then," I remarked.

We all tossed our packs in Jerry's trunk and I got in the front seat. Dan kick started his Triumph, Reno put on the extra riders helmet, hopped on the back, and we all sped off down the alley towards our first order of business. On the way Jerry was wondering about the current state of affairs at my folks.

"Is your old man bugging you about yer' hair?"

"Oh yeah, every day he asks me when I'm going to get it cut."

"And?"

"And I tell him tomorrow."

"Every day?"

"Yep, I say tomorrow every day."

"So how long before you will? Because my old man threatened to kick me out when I grew mine."

"It hasn't come to that yet, and my boss at the foundry doesn't care, so I'm just gonna let it grow."

We pulled in behind Driscoll's chopper at the market and then huddled up on the sidewalk, digging in our pockets. Dan pulled out a wad of bills and looked at each of us.

"Okay, so, at six bucks a case that's a buck-fifty a piece," he said, picking a dollar and change out of his hand. "I think the lady inside must be blind. Every time I've been in there she asks for my I.D. and when I show it to her she looks at it, but then sells to me anyway. I don't think she can see a thing."

"Maybe she sells to you because yer' such a tall handsome devil," Reno laughed. We handed Dan our money and he went inside. Two minutes later he walked out with a large cardboard box of Lucky Lager beer on his shoulder and a big old smile on his face. Jerry quickly opened his trunk and Driscoll carefully set the beer down inside of it.

"Now that we've got the most important thing out of the way, should we hit the B & M next?" Dan asked.

"How about if we get a bucket of KFC?" Jerry offered.

"Sure, sounds good to me," I said.

"That's a great idea!" Reno replied.

"But where're we gonna go?" I asked.

"To KFC, didn't I just say KFC," Jerry refrained. "Jesus MacFarland, are you deaf?"

"No, I mean where are we gonna go after that. Like to a lake or a river somewhere."

"I think we should find some lofty peak to climb," Driscoll proposed, then marched like some soldier up the sidewalk, swinging his arms back and forth, and gazing up at the sky as he turned his head from side to side. He took about six steps away from us then turned around and marched back while we chuckled.

"I ain't gonna go climb a mountain somewhere, if that's what you mean," Reno snapped once Driscoll got back to us.

"Me neither," Jerry added.

"Aw," Dan moaned. "Where's yer' spirit of adventure?"

"Nope, I just want to spend my last weekend before school starts relaxing at some mountain lake, or on a river somewhere," Reno responded.

"Okay, well, how about if we just head up to the mountains and find some trail to a lake?" Driscoll suggested.

"We could head up Stevens Pass, there's lots of lakes and hiking up there. Or we could go up the Stilly?" I mentioned.

"Let's go up Stevens," Driscoll said.

"Yeah, sounds good to me," Jerry replied.

"Sure, that works. I guess," Reno agreed, a touch of reluctance in his voice.

With that Dan mounted his chopper, knocked back the stand with a boot heel and then jumped up in the air and kick started his bike. It roared to life, filling the street with thunder, the sound bouncing off the old clapboard houses of the neighborhood with deafening echoes. Reno hopped on the back and they sped off. Morgan and I piled into his Impala and followed. Five minutes later we were in line at Kentucky Fried Chicken. When it was our turn Reno quickly stepped up to the counter.

"This one's on me, gentlemen," he announced, reaching down into his jeans pocket and pulling out a folded bill.

"Wow! Thanks Reno," we all said at once. He turned around and nodded at us.

"Don't thank me, thank my Mom, she gave me ten bucks this morning."

Soon we were across Broadway at the B & M walking up and down the aisles following Driscoll pushing a shopping cart. He's loaded it with a dozen eggs, bacon, two loaves of bread, cans of chili, pork and beans, corn, a plastic tub of butter, Velveeta cheese, and a box of granola bars. When he stopped in front of the paper plates and towels, he turned around to look at us.

"Did anyone bring anything to cook or eat on besides me?" he asked. Reno and Jerry looked at each other then Reno grinned, "Well, I've got a plate." Morgan shook his head and replied, "I've only got a sleeping bag, but I still have sixty bucks from my last paycheck."

"I've got a skillet and some utensils," I offered.

"Okay, good, I do too," Driscoll replied just as Morgan put a small package of toilet paper in the cart. We all looked down at it.

"That's a damn good idea, Jerry," Reno said to laughter.

At the check-out line I pulled out my wallet and handed Driscoll ten bucks, Jerry did the same. Reno handed him a crumpled wad of dollars and whispered, "Can you get me two packs of Camels." Dan nodded knowing that Steve was still 17 and couldn't buy smokes at the grocery store yet.

With our provisioning done we were off. Driscoll boomed his chopper onto Everett Avenue with Reno on back. Once at Hewitt we all turned to the east and headed out of town. We were city raised kids and hiking pilgrims — ready for just about anything that we could bring upon ourselves. At that point we didn't even know which direction we needed to go except out the Stevens Pass Highway. We knew it was full of hiking and camping opportunities since we'd lived on the edge of the Cascade Mountain Range all our lives, but we still had no final destination in mind when we left Everett and Port Gardner Bay that day.

As Jerry and I barreled across the elevated trestle that went over the farmlands of Ebey Island in his Chevy, it reminded me of all those times before, going out to Lake Stevens or Granite Falls to some backwoods kegger party. When he pushed in the clutch and shifted to speed up so we stayed close to Driscoll it reminded me of one particular summer day a few years before and I flashed back in time.

· · ·

Jerry lived about four blocks north of me. One beautiful sunny morning near the end of August in 1970, just before our sophomore year in high school, I walked down to his house to check on how he was coming along with the re-building of the car he'd bought weeks before. He'd already painted the body yellow, the dash black and installed some cut-rate seat covers. The last time I was there Jerry mentioned that he planned to take out the automatic transmission and change it over to a manual floor shift. He had an older brother Ron, who was a mechanic, and had been coaching him on what to do and how to do it.

When I got to his place he wasn't out in the garage like he usually was so I went up to the house and found the back door open.

"Hey Jerry, you here?"

"Come on in Bobby, everyone's gone."

I walked through the laundry room into the kitchen and just about crapped my pants when I saw him and the table covered in grease and gear oil.

"Criminy, Morgan! What the heck are you doing?!"

"I'm adjusting the shift linkage on the gearbox before I install it. Why? What's it look like?"

There he sat, in his Mom's spotless kitchen, with some filthy, used, wrecking-yard 3-speed transmission sitting on the kitchen table without a single piece of newspaper, cardboard or rag or anything else that would suffice under it. Pools of gear oil that had spilt on the floor were now streaked from him shoving his feet on them not to mention his clothes, hands and table were covered in grime and greasy tools. I couldn't believe my eyes — instantly knowing the trouble I'd be in if I ever pulled a stunt like that in my house.

"Hand me that box-end half inch, would ya'?" he asked, pointing. I saw where it was and picked it up.

"My old man would kill me if I did something like this in my Mom's kitchen," I said, handing him the wrench.

"Aw, don't worry. I'll clean it up," Morgan replied, itching his nose and leaving the outside of his nostril smudged with black.

"Doesn't yer' mom come home at noon?"

"Not today, she's going out to lunch with another lady at her office."

. . .

"Open the glove box," Jerry barked, snapping me out of my day dream. We were slowing down, coming to the small farming community of Snohomish. "I wanna smoke a joint."

"Oh, okay. I'll roll one," I answered, opening the small rectangular door and pulling out a sack of weed and some Zig Zags.

"No, I'm gonna roll it."

"But you're driving."

"I feel like smoking a joint, and I wanna roll it."

"How're you gonna do that and drive?"

"Easy, you steer."

"Me steer while you roll?"

"Yep. Now give me the weed." I knew it was senseless to argue with him so I handed the lid to Jerry, he got to rolling and I grabbed the wheel with my left hand. We came down to the main stoplight in town and could see Driscoll and Reno up ahead of us in the turn lane. When the light changed to green Morgan stepped on the gas and we hit the middle of the intersection way too fast so I couldn't turn the wheel quickly enough.

"Christ MacFarland!" Jerry snapped, dropping the half-rolled joint in the baggie. He quickly took the wheel and finished the turn.

"You went too fast," I replied, grabbing the wheel again as he re-commenced to roll.

At the east end of town he'd finished rolling a sloppy, pregnant joint, shoved it in his mouth and pushed in the dash lighter then handed me the lid to put back in the glove box. A few seconds later the lighter popped out, and we drove through the last stoplight intersection while Jerry began to smoke his sad little bubble of weed. The whole time I was trying to steer and watch the road, when to my great alarm, a logging truck with a huge load of logs was coming the other way just as we started across the Pilchuck River Bridge heading out of town. The semi was crowding the lane, Morgan was puffing away on his hapless joint, and I couldn't quite get a proper read of the road with smoke filling my eyes. I eased the car over to the right to stay clear of the logging truck but I ended up over-steering so the right front tire hit the concrete curb. The car did a little jump-hop, "CHRIST!" Jerry hollered, the joint fell out of his mouth, and the truck driver laid on his horn and Jake-brake, blasting the be-Jesus out of us with the sound of impending doom!

"HOLY SHIT! MacFarland!" Morgan yelled. The car was bouncing and swerving around, the hot joint was now down between his legs burning a hole in his cheap imitation-leather seat covers, and I was trying to keep us on the road. Finally, Morgan grabbed the wheel, glanced down and found the refer, picked it out from between his legs, put it back in his mouth and started to brush the embers and ash onto the floor with his fingers.

"I told ya' that wasn't a good idea."

"Christ! You just about got us killed!" Jerry barked, giving me the stink eye.

"The hell I did! That wouldn't have happened if you woulda' let me roll."

"Yeah, well," he said, his voice fading, sucking on his sad, bent little doobie, getting the ember to burn again. He took a huge toke and handed it out for me.

"Nah, that's okay. I'll wait until we get to where we're going."

Once at Gold Bar we saw far ahead that Driscoll had pulled over at the town's little general store, so we did too. By the time we piled out of the Impala Reno had a lit Camel in his mouth and was standing in front of the outdoor bulletin board while Dan was already inside. Jerry and I walked in and the first thing I noticed was the multiple strings of colored lights hanging from the ceiling then the racks of canned goods, boxes of sundries and household items, camping gear, fishing poles and tackle and everything else you could imagine from the floor to the rafters — the counter had barely enough room to put anything on it.

An overweight old-timer sporting a big white bushy beard, rosy cheeks and red nose wearing a green flannel shirt was sitting behind it with a white Meerschaum pipe in his mouth billowing smoke. He's the personification of hillbilly Christmas all year long but greeted us with a suspicious smirk and a wary eye as we ambled in with our long hair and patched jeans. Jerry immediately started latching onto candy bars and a package of chips, Driscoll had found a county road map on the wall.

"Any good places to hike around here?" Dan asked, looking over at the old-timer. Saint Nick took the pipe from his mouth, set it in a large ashtray and slowly began to stand up from his chair.

"Good Lord, if I had a dollar for every time I've been asked that over the last 30 years, why, I'd be a rich man livin' in a big house on the river instead of behind this place," he remarked, strolling over with a little half-step waddle to the map while staring at Driscoll.

"So! We've got the Wallace Falls trail up above town, the Big and Little Heart Lake trail near Sky, and Delta Lake above the Foss, but my all-time favorite is Blanca up Index way. There's more beauty at Lake Blanca than heaven can hold — now that's a fact."

"Lake Blanca, huh?" Driscoll replied, trying to find it on the map. Just then Reno walked in and went straight to the cooler, pulling out a can of cola.

"Here, let me show ya'," the old man said, stepping over in front of the map and finding it for Driscoll. "Just head on up the highway to Index and then take the North Fork Road past town for about ten 'er so miles, go past Troublesome Creek Campground, and then take the Forest Service road where it says Lake Blanca Trailhead."

"You've been up there?" Reno asked, inserting himself into the conversation.

"Why yes, son, I have. Many times. But I must say, it's been a few years. Immaculate untouched emerald-green water, giant fir trees, snowcapped peaks, and there's even a glacier at the far end with two waterfalls that flow over a granite cliff as tall as the Space Needle! Such beauty the good Lord has provided us. And just a stone's throw to the north is Monte Cristo. You boys ever been up to

Monte? You know, a fella can still drive there, well, ya' can from the Granite Falls side, that is."

"Lake Blanca sounds good, and yes, we did a night at Monte Cristo back when I was a Scout," Driscoll answered. "How long of a hike is it?"

The old-timer gazed up at the ceiling while scratching the side of his bearded face, he paused to contemplate an answer and then ruminated, "Oh, it ain't bad fer' a bunch a fella's yer' age. Why, I bet you youngsters could run up there and back today, easy!"

"We were planning to spend two nights, somewhere," Reno offered.

"No problem then boys. If'n I was yer' age why I'd shut down this place and join ya'."

"That does sound good, doesn't it?" I said. "Waterfalls and glaciers seems just like what we're lookin' for."

Meanwhile, Morgan had his wallet out with a pile of munchies on the counter. He was about ready to tear open one of the three candy bars he wanted to buy when I looked up at a clock on the wall that read 1:30.

"We need to get going. Is it Blanca then?"

"Blanca it is," Driscoll agreed.

"Well, okay," Reno grumbled forlornly, walking over to the counter with his pop.

"Thanks mister," Jerry said after paying, then went outside with Dan.

"See you outside," I mentioned to them, stepping over next to Reno. The rack of cigars behind the counter caught my eye.

"Those, um, Swishers, how much are they?"

"Ninty-five cents for a pack of five," the old timer replied, handing Steve his change.

"They any good?" I asked as Reno left.

"Like smokin' molasses, son. Have ya' got I.D. showin' yer' 18?"

"I do," I answered, reaching for my wallet.

"That's okay, I believe ya'," he said, raising up a hand. "But if'n ya' smoke a whole pack on a Saturday night ya' better be ready to redeem yerself an' sit in a pew to confess yer' sins come Sunday mornin'." I smiled and put a dollar bill on the counter as he set down a pack of them.

"I'll keep that in mind. Thanks again."

Outside Reno had shoved a quarter in a newspaper machine and was in the process of opening the door and taking out a weekend edition of the Seattle P-I. He carried the thick paper over to a garbage can, started taking all the advertisement sections out and tossing them. Once done he walked over to the back of the Impala while Dan and I watched as Morgan opened his trunk. Reno shoved his can of pop and the now folded newspaper into his net pack, picked it up, flung it over his shoulder and strapped it on instead of putting it back into the trunk. He looked at us, his eyebrow raised and then opened his mouth.

"What?"

"Do you really need that paper?" Driscoll asked, strolling over to his bike.

"All I wanna do this weekend is relax by some lake and read the latest crap about that rat-bastard Nixon and his Watergate goons."

"You and your politics can relax all you want once we get to where we're going," he replied, raising his right leg and straddling his chopper.

"Yeah, well, once we need to get a campfire going you won't have to look too far for some starter material!" Reno said, grinning. With that Driscoll kick started his chopper to life, Reno hopped on the back, and Jerry and I piled into the car and we headed on up the highway. As we pulled away I chuckled to myself at the sight of Reno's see-through netting poor man's backpack showing his porcelain plate and newspaper.

We zoomed past a lumber mill and over the high bridge spanning the Skykomish River, it felt like we were flying since we were so far above the water and trees below. Next we cruised past Zeke's Drive-In then came into view of Mount Index — it rose up before us like a giant monolith of majesty with massive fingers of granite pointing straight up to the heavens. The road twisted around bends, went up and down hills, crossed another bridge and we took a turn towards the village of Index. A mile later we rolled past the little town on the other side of the river and continued up the North Fork Road that followed the Skykomish.

Soon we were surrounded by a dense rain forest of soft and hardwoods, the moss covered hemlocks and firs so thick they blocked out the sun. A natural canopy of vine maple and evergreen limbs reached out over the paved county road only allowing brief shafts of golden sunshine to seep through. The forest floor was carpeted with moss and tall bushy ferns, it felt like we were traveling through a Hobbit-like landscape of fairy tale stories. We drove past cabins and over multiple short bridges spanning streams that came crashing down from the mountains above us and caught glimpses of lofty peaks in the distance.

Up ahead, Driscoll slowed down and then pulled over near a Forest Service campground sign that read "Troublesome Creek." We rolled up beside him and could see down into the camping area that it was packed full of trailers and people there for the Labor Day weekend.

"How we doing?" Driscoll yelled, trying to be heard over the rumbling idle of his bike.

"So far so good," I replied. "Nice scenery. I'd love to live up here someday."

"Looks like all of America's out this weekend," Driscoll remarked, tilting his head towards the campground.

"Let's just stay here!" Reno hollered. "Looks fine by me."

"No way O'Riley," Jerry hollered through my window. "I'm not gonna waste my weekend listening to a bunch of bratty screamin' little kids being yelled at by their parents."

"Yeah, I think we need Blanca! It's just up ahead!" Driscoll barked, revving his engine. He smiled a wicked grin, roared off up the road and we followed.

Just past the campground the road changed to gravel, then dirt, and began to climb. Driscoll turned left at a trailhead sign and the road got steeper but soon it leveled out and we came to a small crude parking lot with three cars at it.

Driscoll parked and shut down his chopper but kept his helmet on, Jerry and I got out of the car. We ambled over to them as Dan started to walk around with his hands on his hips while scanning the immediate area.

"Whatcha looking for?" I asked, wandering over to him.

"Well, uh, I haven't wired my bike with a key start yet, just a toggle switch, so anyone could start it and steal it if they wanted to. I'm thinking that I should stash it out in the woods."

Looking around I could see that we were located in a steep mountain valley. One side was a straight-up timbered hillside the other was fairly flat with a short but not too steep cut-bank at the edge of the parking area that rose to a piece of ground and looked level. Driscoll saw it too, he scrambled up the bank to scout the terrain. After a quick look-see he came back to the edge and stuck two broken-off pieces of limb into the ground about ten feet apart then scrambled down the short hill.

"What's the plan?" I asked. Reno took off his backpack and leaned against Jerry's car with him.

"I'm gonna run my bike up that bank," Driscoll said, motioning towards it, "and hide it up there in those woods where it's out of sight."

"You're gonna take a run up that embankment?" Reno asked, cackling.

"No problem," Driscoll replied.

"Impossible," Reno snickered.

"He can do it," Jerry said, smiling.

"This I gotta see!" O'Riley quipped.

I knew Driscoll had spent a good deal of his youth riding dirt bikes, plus he had rebuilt his current ride starting with just its frame, so I silently grinned at Reno's remark knowing full well that Dan could easily run his bike right on up the side of that bank and into those woods. Driscoll turned around, strolled over to his chopper and started it, the roar of the bike echoed though the valley and seemed to bounce off the surrounding cliffs.

He stomped his left boot heel on the shifter, dropping it into gear, slowly let out the clutch and turned around, then goosed it and zoomed back down the way we came. Once he was about forty yards away he turned around and stopped. He tightened the chin strap on his helmet, revved the engine and then popped the clutch. Seconds later he was roaring up the dirt road, he stood up on the pegs, made a slight turn and zoomed up the embankment right between his two pieces of wood and was airborne, flying into the trees like some daredevil in a circus. The last thing we saw was the brake light disappearing into the trees. Jerry and I whooped with approving calls while Reno stood slack-jawed and bug-eyed, slightly bent forward with his arms hanging straight down.

A moment later Driscoll killed the engine, we saw him walking out to the edge of the bank with his hands over his head like he'd scored a touchdown.

"Way to go!" Jerry yelled. "I knew you could do it! Just like Evil Knievel!"

"Evil Knievel?!" an astounded Reno replied. "Hell, he's Dangerous Dan Driscoll!" And we all howled with laughter. "I can't believe it, shit! He's Dangerous Dan from here on out as far as I'm concerned!" Reno hollered, sounding like a converted believer.

"Yeah, yeah," Driscoll answered, then beckoned with his hand. "Can you guys come up here and help me find some tree limbs and stuff to cover the bike with?"

"Sure," we all answered at once and climbed up the bank. A few minutes later we'd found enough brush to cover the chopper so it was completely concealed and Driscoll was satisfied. On the way back down Dan pulled the two upright pieces of limb and swept the dirt his tire tracks had made on the cut-bank to hide them and we were ready to head to the lake.

I looked at my watch and was surprised to see that it was almost 3:00 in the afternoon, I hadn't realized we were already that far into our day. We started to ready ourselves and divvyed up the food between our backpacks. Morgan slung his sleeping bag over his neck and decided to hand carry the case of beer while Reno strapped on his see-through back pack and grabbed the bucket of chicken.

"I've got some extra room in my pack for the KFC," Driscoll offered, looking at Reno.

"Nope, I bought it, so I'm carrying it," O'Riley quickly answered, a sly grin on his face. With his head of frizzy hair, faded and frayed blue jeans, and the netting pack on his back he looked like some kind of urban hippie tennis Sherpa freak.

"Okay! Onward we go, gentlemen," Driscoll said, shouldering his pack and taking the lead with Reno and Jerry right behind him while I brought up the rear.

So we were off. We had no map, no compass, and no idea of what we were in for. Even though we may have been lacking in critical wilderness equipment we had no absence of desire. After finding the trailhead we made a start, thinking it was going to be a wonderful walk in the woods. About a-hundred yards up the trail we saw an older, grey-haired couple coming down and I said to myself, *"if they've been up to the lake and back today then this should be easy."*

"Afternoon," Reno said, greeting them, "How's things up at Lake Blanca?" They glanced at the bucket of chicken Steve was carrying as he ambled by them — then they turned and gawked at his tennis netting back pack and wild bushy hair. Jerry walked by them next with the case of beer and the look on their faces changed from astonishment to confused bewilderment.

"Oh, we just went up to the cliffs for lunch today," the woman replied, continuing down to the parking area.

"Good luck, fellas," the man said over his shoulder as I walked by him.

The trail began to get steep and we zig-zagged on switchbacks that wound back and forth through old growth Douglas fir. Twenty minutes into the hike Morgan was getting tired lugging the beer so he sat down on a boulder and Reno joined him.

"Break time!" Jerry loudly moaned, breathing hard and setting down the box.

"How much farther do you think it is?" O'Riley asked, catching his breath.

"Oh, I'd say about three and a half miles, more or less," Driscoll answered. "Didn't you see that little number 4 on the trailhead sign?"

"Miles?! I thought that was the trail number," Steve snapped. "Three more miles. I knew we should have just stayed down at that campground."

"Trail number?! Hah! That's a good one!" Driscoll laughed. "If those old folks could make it up there you can too, Reno. Come on, yer' slowing us down!"

Steve and Jerry stood up and we started out again. Dan once more took the lead, he began to pull away and got ahead of us. A quarter mile later we started to get separated so I stopped, put my hands to the side of my mouth and yelled.

"Dan! Can you hear me?! Slow down!"

"Okay!" he yelled back.

There were still more switchbacks, the trail seemed to be indifferent to our plight. We kept going higher and higher and I began to creep ahead of Jerry and Reno. At one switchback there was a cliff twenty feet past the turn with a large windfall log back from the edge with huckleberry bushes surrounding it. I walked over to it and the views were astounding. A deep rocky gorge was before me, towering jagged peaks rose up from the other side. I picked a few berries to enjoy and said to myself, *"This might be where the cou-*

ple was for their lunch." So I sat down and started to devour more huckleberries.

Five minutes later I heard voices coming up the trail — it was Reno and Jerry bitching. "What are we doing all the way up here?" And, "I knew we should have stayed down below." Too finally, "I shoulda just stayed home and worked on my car." I stood up when I could see them.

"Hey! Over here, there's a great place to sit down," I offered, waving them over.

"Christ, this is beginning to be a bit much," Reno said, plodding up and sitting down.

"No shit," Jerry added, taking the beer down from his shoulder. "What time is it anyway?"

"Going on five," I answered, looking at my watch.

While the two of them took a breather I strolled up the trail twenty yards and called out.

"Driscoll! Hello? Dan, Driscoll!" But there was no reply and I thought, *"This is not good."*

I turned around and walked back to them and there sat Morgan opening up a beer and diving into the chicken. *"Oh no, he's done, that's it for him."* Then I noticed Reno had cracked open his can of pop and was reaching for a drumstick so I grabbed one too.

"Okay, I'm going to run ahead and slow Driscoll down," I told them, taking a bite. "But don't sit too long. It's gonna start to get dark in a couple of hours." Both Reno and Jerry just nodded so I turned around and hit the trail with earnest.

Twenty-minutes later I was beginning to get worried and found myself counting steps to take my mind off our little collective predicament, I'd count to fifty and then start again. I kept stopping to yell for Dan but got nothing in response. The trail seemed to keep growing in front of me and I thought, *"Good God, are we hiking to hell or hiking to Nirvana?"*

Soon I found myself in a rhythmic kind of detachment trying to concentrate on putting one foot in front of the other, catching myself from falling over with each step because my backpack was beginning to get heavy, sweat was dripping down my face and getting in my eyes. All I could do was keep my head down and my feet moving. I stopped and yelled back to Steve and Jerry, but there was no response. *"We are, IDIOTS! Christ! We should be trying to stay together!"*

I just kept hiking and hiking, figuring that since Jerry and Reno had something to eat and drink they'd be okay, and kept heading up the trail to try to find Driscoll. Higher and farther, and it's all uphill, no breaks. It just kept going and going when the trees opened up and I could see a short ridge with a snowfield at the top. *"When on earth is this going to end? Snow! For the love of God!"* Dusk was coming down on the mountains, I was about to sit down and give up when I heard someone yelling.

"Hello, Bobby?! Hello Reno?! Jerry?!"

"Dan! Is that you?" I hollered back.

Finally! Boy was I relieved. I climbed as fast as I could up to the top of the snowfield and there was Driscoll down below waving his arms at the bottom of the snow covered hill. What a sight for sore eyes he was! He yelled back about Steve and Jerry so I told him that they were still down the trail. I walked down to him and there was the lake back away from us; it wasn't quite what old St. Nick in Gold Bar had described, it was really small. By then Driscoll had his backpack off and was rummaging around in it, eventually finding the Velveeta. As I watched him dig around I spied the top of a glass bottle in a side pocket.

"Is that a pint of whiskey?" I asked. He jerked his head around and grinned.

"It is, I had my neighbor buddy get it for me. But don't tell Reno or Jerry, I wanna save it for tomorrow night."

"Okay, no problem. So, that's Lake Blanca?" I asked, pointing behind him.

"I guess," Dan replied, tearing the foil off the package of cheese. He sat down on a log and then sliced off a big hunk with his pocket knife and offered it to me.

"Thanks." It felt like we'd been sent on some wild goose chase. I sat down next to him and we ate Velveeta and talked about how screwed up we were because darkness was coming over the woods. We were beginning to really worry about what we should do next when we heard Reno's voice.

"Hello?! Anybody around?!"

"Here, down here!" we yelled back and waved our arms. Gawd, what an enormous relief it was to see their two silhouettes at the top of the snowfield. Jerry instantly set the case of beer down on the snow, sat on it, and then slid down like he's a kid on a sled. Reno followed him on his ass and they both came to a stop in front of us, then slowly stood up. Right away we noticed that Reno had used the KFC bucket for his sled. He stood up with it in his grip, crushed and empty.

"Looks like you guys made quick work of the chicken," I remarked. They both did a double take and chuckled.

"Sorry," Steve grinned, holding up the collapsed container, "We were very hungry."

"Well," Driscoll laughed, "We just ate half the cheese." But there was plenty of beer left so we each had one sitting there on our log wallowing in our situation but still glad to have made it. We ambled over to the tiny lake and buried the beer in a patch of nearby snow. At the edge of the pond in a grove of trees was a dug out fire pit ringed with rocks.

"That's Lake Blanca?" Reno asked, taking off his net pack and setting it down. "I busted my butt to get all the way up here and this is what I get! Jaysus! That guy at the store sent us on a snipe hunt!"

"Where's all the emerald green water and glaciers?" Jerry moaned, tossing his sleeping bag on the ground next to the fire pit. "Did we make a wrong turn back there somewhere?"

"I don't think so," Driscoll responded, taking off his rucksack and slapping the back of his neck. He slapped the back of his neck again and then Jerry slapped his arm. A squadron of mosquitoes began bombarding us and we had no escape.

"Great! Just great! Lake Blanca is a bug infested pond!" Reno complained, slapping the side of his face, killing one. "These things are huge! Anyone got some bug spray?"

"None here."

"Me neither."

"Don't look at me."

"We need to get a big old white-man fire going! Now!" Driscoll ordered, as we all immediately peeled off in search of firewood. Fifteen minutes later the woods were dark, the stars were out and Reno had taken the newspaper out of his ad-hoc pack and started crumpling up some of it for fire starter, a lit cigarette dangling from his mouth, then began to pile small bits of limbs and twigs on the paper.

"I knew this newspaper would be a good idea," he said.

"I'm gonna take a stab and guess that's the sports page yer' using," I retorted.

"You guessed right."

Driscoll walked up with a huge armload of wood and dropped it at the edge of the fire pit. All of us were slapping and flailing at bugs, I breathed one in and spat it out.

"For criminy sakes, this is worse than Lake Wenatchee last June! Remember?" I asked.

"Yeah, that was bad, wasn't it?" Driscoll replied.

"I thought they were gonna carry us off at one point," Jerry said.

"These things are like 747s," Reno added, striking a match and lighting the paper. Soon we had a roaring fire going and the bugs began to leave us alone.

We didn't have tents but Driscoll had his hammock so he dug it out of his pack and started to string it up between two close-by trees while the rest of us rolled out our sleeping bags on the ground and collapsed on top of them, dog-tired, dead asleep in no time.

• • •

The next morning we awoke to the sound of Driscoll swatting mosquitoes and swearing up a blue streak. He's cussing, jerking around inside of his bag, and as he does we slowly started snickering while we watched a massive cloud of mosquitoes land on him hanging in his hammock. When he moved, the mosquitoes flew off, but when he was still, they landed back on him. Driscoll was not a very happy camper. He finally gave up, rolled out of his hammock, fell to the ground with a thud and a collective laugh from the rest of us. For some reason the mosquitoes had decided to really go after him, but only nibble on us.

We got a fire going and had a hearty breakfast of scrambled eggs, bacon and fried bread with butter. Since we were a little haggard we went for a morning swim in the pond, which was very refreshing. After our tranquil mountain breakfast and pond water bath, Reno pulled out his newspaper, sat up against a tree and diligently began to read the latest reporting on the Watergate scandal. I could hear him muttering angrily, something to the effect of, "we gotta nail this criminal bastard," then slapping the page with the back of his hand.

The rest of us continued to relax by our private little Lake Blanca when about thirty serene minutes of mountain quietude later some hikers showed up. They were all wearing fancy hiking clothes and had new backpacks with metal frames, using ski poles for walking sticks, two men and two women.

"Good morning," Reno said to them, looking up from his paper, striking up a conversation. They stopped and glanced around at us and our sad little hobo camp. Steve got up and walked over to them.

"That's one heck of a climb to get up here, huh?" Reno remarked.

"Oh, it's a good workout, that's for sure," one man replied, grinning. "So, how come you're camping here?" the same guy asked, a quizzical look forming on his face.

"Well, why not?" Reno questioned back.

"Because Lake Blanca is only about a-quarter mile away, just down the trail," he answered, straight faced and pointing.

"So . . . this isn't Blanca?"

"No this is Virgin Lake. We were up here last year," the other guy in the group said. When the fellow said, "last year," the look on Steve's face transformed to astonishment and his cheeks took on a slightly blushed tone, he must have realized that they had labored up the side of a mountain for fun, two years in a row.

"Oh, okay, thank you," Reno quickly replied, and they strolled off to where the trail continued, which we hadn't even noticed that morning, and disappeared. We all looked at each other and about fell down howling. Here we were — a gaggle of virgin Cascade wilderness hikers camping at Virgin Lake!

"*Jaysus!* Are we a bunch of numbskulls or what?" Reno cracked, and we all shared another collective laugh.

"Should we pack everything up and move down to the lake?" I asked out loud, glancing around at our messy little situation.

"Fine by me, all I've got is my sleeping bag," Jerry said.

"Nah, let's just go for the day and then come back. Besides, we've got all that beer over there covered in snow," Reno mentioned, pointing towards our booze stash.

"Forgot about the beer," Jerry groaned, "I don't feel like lugging it around again even though we still have the box."

"Well, our beer and stuff should be fine. I don't think anyone's gonna steal it," Driscoll mentioned.

"Sounds good to me but I'm gonna need something to eat before we head out," Jerry suggested.

"Me too," I added.

"What?" Reno quipped, raising his arms as if alarmed, "You mean to tell me it's your feeding time again, already?"

"That's right," Jerry replied. "How'd you think I got so tall?"

"Well, I could go for something to eat, especially if we're gonna spend the day there," Driscoll added.

So we ate cheese sandwiches, Reno included, and then headed for the real Lake Blanca. We found the dirt trail, it began to descend and changed from duff to gravel then sharp rocks as we walked through a thick forest of towering fir trees. Soon the old-growth timberland began to thin and the lake emerged from almost out of nowhere; a pristine, untouched natural world opened up before us. It was exhilarating, and like seeing the environment through an unfiltered wide-angle lens with child-like eyes.

The lake water had a deep translucent aquamarine tone and rested in a basin ringed by mountains with steep rock fields that dropped down to the waterline. The trail came in where a large creek drained it. An enormous logjam of hundreds of dead trees clogged the outlet, logs with their root systems still attached covered the flowing water. Driscoll stepped out onto one and walked the length of it.

"It's solid," he said, "I can see more logs submerged underneath. I wonder if this is Troublesome Creek." He got down on his knees, splashed some water on his face then cupped his hands and took a few slurps.

"Good!" he yelled, smiling back at us. We joined him and it was like drinking from the purest wishing well ever known to mankind; clear and cold. A minute later everyone got up and crossed over to the other side while I hung back for a moment and enjoyed more of the ale of the earth. After I'd quenched my thirst I rejoined the group.

At the far end in the distance there was a tall twin water fall coming from a glacier, it dropped over a massive cliff landing on a rock field that was flanked by glacial-till sediment and then cascaded to the lake. High above it snowcapped peaks loomed — their craggy flanks and cliffs dropped down to the water giving it the appearance of a Norwegian fjord. A living-color high mountain picture postcard was before us and we were overtaken with the beauty. Just like that, old St. Nick at the Gold Bar store became our friend, instead of the brunt of our collective disdain.

There were only the hikers from the morning, who were now setting up tents on the opposite side of the lake and two other tents up-lake from them, but we couldn't see anyone else around. Beauty was definitely ours as we strolled the shoreline and took in the views. While we were walking Driscoll spotted a granite hill up ahead that rose out of the water, which climbed a couple hundred feet and then flattened out on top.

"Hey, let's go climb that!" he hollered, pointing at it.

"We should! That looks like nothing compared to what we did yesterday," I said.

"No way! What do you two think you are now, huh? Mountain climbers?!" Reno exclaimed.

"We should do it. The views have got to be killer from up there," Jerry added.

So the majority ruled, we started up the side of the mini-mountain and finally got to the summit winded, but relieved and glad to be in one piece. We sat down and caught our breath in a small meadow of beautiful wild flowers, foliage and moss covered rocks and stubbly grasses. While we were taken aback with the surroundings Driscoll pulled out his wallet and started searching inside of it.

"Dan," Reno said, "You don't need to pay for anything up here."

"Yes, well," he replied, "That may be true, but I thought we might need a little extra something to heighten the experience. If you know what I mean?" He took a small photo packet out of his wallet and held it up towards the rest of us, we saw two hits of blotter acid.

"Well I'll be damned!" Reno exclaimed. "Where'd you get that?"

"Oh, I've got my sources," he answered, a sly grin forming on his face. "I had some of this stuff last weekend and a half hit will give you a perfect little body stone, nothing serious."

"This is turning out to be one hell of a hike after all!" Jerry added. Driscoll pulled his pocket knife from his trousers and began to slice the two hits in half on top of the photo packet, just like it was meant for such an undertaking and presto. He handed each of us our portion and in turn we downed the acid.

A minute later Morgan started rolling one of his sloppy pregnant reefers, lit it up and we sucked in some of nature's own herb to enjoy our mountain meadow top experience. Reno walked over to the edge of the cliff and sat down cross legged, taking his ease. I laid on my side and gazed at our surroundings.

Ten minutes later my teeth and gums began to tingle — the sensation moved through my jaw then extended to my whole body. I rolled over and stared at the flowers, tiny blue Daisies, blue Larkspur and white 3-leaf Trillium with little yellow fingers jutting out from their blossoms — they began to slowly move and grow taller, the petals got larger and then their colors turned a vivid Day-Glow florescent of blue, green, yellow and red. I lost myself in a moment of time-lapse transcendental bliss.

I blinked my eyes and glanced over at the twin waterfall — the shimmering cascade of water changed to falling diamonds that eventually splashed onto the emerald surface of the lake, the sparkling rolling water was like jewels piling up, when, like a scene in a dream that you never want to end, the waterfalls changed to liquid silver that flowed over the cliff smooth and shinning, dropping to a granite bathtub cauldron of boiling bright metal. My mind was swimming in delight as I gazed in endorphin heaven when a few seconds later the outline of the lake returned, its quicksilver changing back to water again.

Smiling, I turned to view the flowers and now I could smell them. A wonderful, natural perfume filled my senses — sweet luscious scents rose up like notes of pizzicato music and I found myself weightless, suspended above the ground in a brief moment of floating contentment that I'd never experienced before. I closed my eyes and allowed my existence to hover above the sweet aroma for a few moments.

All too soon my body started to feel thick and solid with weight. Opening my eyes I returned to earth and the miracle of wonder touched my soul, I felt as if I'd been baptized in Mother Earth's womb. I realized how delicate the natural world was and how the human race needed to eliminate the polluting of our wonderful planet. Altruistic thoughts of saving the earth from greedy industrialists splintered my mind in sharp relief when in a stunning life-changing moment I recognized that our planet was created to be a life source and not a resource for industrialists to exploit. *"It's a source for life, not a resource, but a source for infinite life,"* and my body buzzed with the warm sense of earthly affirmation.

A nano-second later I came to the understanding that the human race should not treat the natural world as something that was separate from ourselves. I saw the world from a completely different vantage point than just minutes before and realized that the natural world and the human race were one. It was like seeing everything through a new prism that pointed me in the direction of helping to save our environment. I was completely overtaken with a transformative eco-conscious experience just as the piercing sound of a loud voice interrupted my profoundly escalating travels of enlightenment via psychedelia.

"How in the hell are we gonna get down off-a this thing?" Reno blurted.

"Good question," Jerry replied, standing up. "Because I sure as shit ain't gonna go back down the way we came up."

I snapped out of my day dream and pushed myself up on my haunches. "Are you guys feeling that stuff yet?" I asked, thinking I'd gotten more than they did.

"Just a touch," Jerry answered.

"I've got a good little body buzz goin'," Reno replied.

"Feeling alright here," Driscoll added, grinning like a Cheshire cat. "We'll just head back this way," he said, pointing behind us.

So Dan turned into the Boy Scout he once was and took charge, leading us back away from the lake, as I tripped and stumbled along behind them — taking in all the plants and birds of the forest, beautifully lost in my life-affirming, planet saving acid journey.

We came upon a single towering old-growth Douglas fir, it climbed up to the heavens with thick fibrous bark that looked like a kind of natural armor. I stopped to look up the massive tree and saw it as a grand monument, then smiled with the thought that no timber company industrialist would ever harvest it being so far out in the wilderness. We skirted around its wide girth and found our way through heavy brush, to the shore and then back to our little hobo camp. Once there, we found that nothing had been messed with and we were starving, so we got a camp fire going then broke out a few beers and had a before dinner reefer, to get the attitude right for what felt like was going to be a mile-high meal.

Collectively we had a notion that the best thing to do was dump our cans of chili and pork and beans into one pot for a giant feast. We were feeling fine as dusk began to come over the woods, the fire crackled while we piled up stray branches in anticipation of a roaring bonfire that night. Once there was a good bed of coals our stomachs rumbled with hunger, then Dan poured our canned cuisine into his lone cook pot. I in turn dug out the package of Swishers from my backpack, lit one, and then passed them around for everyone to smoke and enjoy.

As we chatted about the day and puffed our cigars we didn't take notice that Driscoll had placed a spoon in the pot, to stir our meal. While we waited for our mulligan to boil Reno delighted us with stories of old childhood friends, as we drank snow cold beer. O'Riley was spinning tall tales while we chuckled with laughter — the light of the fire was like a torch illuminating us and the surrounding trees, the sparks rising up to a few faint stars and a wonderful crescent moon.

Reno's stories kept coming and coming, with his hands wringing and eyes glistening. As I listened to Steve weave some fantastical fiction about how his oldest brother had caught the biggest salmon in Puget Sound history I saw him as a kind of cross between Ernest Hemingway and Alan King. I determined that he was the social vanguard and lead vocalist of our group, he was always on point. Reno was in fine storytelling form when Driscoll reached down to stir the pot. He grabbed the long sitting spoon and —

"Holy H . . . Roosevelt Christ!" he hollered at the top of his lungs, pulling his hand back from the pot. Dan started jumping up and down, shaking his hand and cursing the hot spoon then ran over to the pond to put his hand in the cold water, so we followed.

We hovered over him in silence with baited breath waiting for his hand to cool, he pulled it from the pond, and we looked. On his right index finger we could see the letters 'Made in the USA,' backwards, in black burnt skin. We didn't know whether to laugh or cry for him, and when he started to laugh, we did too. Driscoll held out his finger and we looked again, and sure enough, there in burnt black were the letters with the outline of the spoons edge seared into his finger, like a tattoo.

"Holy crap," I said. "Are you okay?"

"Oh," Dan replied, "I'll be fine, good thing I've got some whiskey to kill the pain."

"Whiskey! You've got whiskey?" Reno blurted. "Why you dirty dog, you've been holdin' out on us, huh?"

Chuckling, we went back to the fire only to find that our last supper had been dumped over from Dan quickly pulling his hand from the pot, our meal was now sizzling in a drowned out coals and ruined. Our laughter quickly subsided but soon enough we were glancing back and forth at each other, started shaking our heads, and then began laughing at our sorry situation.

Driscoll was in pain so he went over to his back pack, found the pint of liquor and took a couple of huge swigs. He walked back to the drizzled out embers of the former campfire, took another belt, poured a touch of whiskey on his finger, and finally handed the bottle to O'Riley.

"Here ya' go Steve-a-Reno. Nothin' like a little of the brown to ease the pain," he said.

"Well, thank you, Dangerous Dan," Reno replied with his wry Irish grin.

Driscoll and I went over to our packs to look for a few morsels of food, anything to eat. Luckily we found one more can of pork and beans, a can of corn, and a few granola bars. It wasn't much, but just barely enough to sooth our palates. We got another fire going to begin cooking our meager meal while we sat around the campfire listening to Steve.

With every sip of whiskey Reno chased it with a swig of beer and soon his stories no longer cut through the night air with their previous clarity. Sitting cross legged at the edge of the fire he was nattering away then paused to take a pull of brown liquor and started laughing so hard at one of his own jokes before he even told it that he spit a spray of whiskey out in the air over the campfire. It ignited a flash of blazing flames that instantly shot back to his lips! Alarmed and blinded by whiskey fueled fire, he instantly fell back on the ground, in so doing the bottle flew in the air, and Reno started flailing wildly at his face virtually like a man on fire as we burst into side splitting hilarity. The bottle landed on a near-by boulder and shattered to pieces.

"JAYSUS!" Reno hollered, lying on his back. "That never happened before!"

"I guess that's to be expected from a wild man drunk on fire water and high on acid!" Driscoll cracked, laughing.

"Shit Reno, you looked like a fire breathing crazy man at a circus!" I said, standing up to help him get back on his feet.

"Either that or Evil Knievel!" Morgan added, giggling uncontrollably, rolling back and forth on the ground.

"Yeah, who's the dangerous daredevil now?" Driscoll said, and we all howled at the moon.

• • •

The next morning our bellies rumbled with hunger and like a gaggle of starved, hung-over laggards, we began to break camp. As I rolled up my sleeping bag I flashed on the absolute thought of leaving nothing behind. After I'd tied the bag to my pack I started to collect the empty beer bottles and picked up the shattered pieces of glass from the pint of whiskey.

"Whatcha doin'?" Jerry asked.

"We've gotta pack out all our shit, can't leave anything behind. If we packed it in, we're packin' it out!" I said loudly, setting the beer box cardboard and leftover KFC bucket in the fire pit and striking a match.

Driscoll instantly pulled a hooded sweatshirt out from his rucksack and tied the sleeves together, making a make-shift garbage bag, and we began to fill it with all the cans and bottles but in no time it was overfilled. So I found a t-shirt in my backpack and placed it over the rest of the bottles, broke them with a rock, then wrapped up all the glass in the shirt and put it in my pack. With that Driscoll and I shouldered our packs, Reno strapped on his overflowing with garbage Sherpa hippie net pack, and we hit the trail.

We made our way back up the snowfield and then down the route, but this time we stayed together and were able to finally enjoy a somewhat relaxing but starved for sustenance walk in the woods.

As we hiked I felt like I had a new purpose in life, and that even if we started out just two days before with no map or compass to guide us I'd found solace in a new internal chart to point me in the right direction to follow, an ecological design to help save our planet. Good feelings welled up inside of me that masked the emptiness in my belly.

Once we got down to the parking lot Driscoll kept walking across the road while he took off his rucksack, set it down, and scrambled up the bank. A minute later we heard the sound of his chopper roaring back to life and then there was Dan straddled on his bike, easing over the bank and down to the road.

We got loaded up and headed back the way we came with Driscoll and Reno in the lead. At the town of Index Dan turned and roared across the river bridge. We pulled up to the general store and walked over to the door but it was locked!

"Crap," Reno said, pushing on the entrance. "They're closed."

"Oh, that's right. Labor Day," Driscoll remarked.

"Damn it," Jerry added. "I'm starving."

"Well, let's hope Zeke's is open," I said. We all piled into and onto our respective rides and zoomed away.

Ten minutes later we pulled into the Drive-In's parking lot, it was jam packed with tons of tourists with their trailers and kids and there was a very long line at the order window. We scurried over to the end of the queue with our bellies rumbling. The line had barely moved after what seemed like hours, we were about ready to break down the backdoor and start grilling burgers on our own.

Finally, we got our order in and found a picnic table behind the place near a cedar tree and sat down bone-tired, and famished. Order numbers were being called out over an outdoor speaker and smiling people were carrying trays of food to tables as we watched in heavy anticipation.

"Too bad we're not at the Woodsman right now," Jerry mentioned. "Because I could sure go for a nice juicy steak smothered in onions with a baked potato."

"Well, seeing how we're about forty miles away from the Woodsman I guess you're just gonna have to settle for a cheeseburger and fries for the time being," Reno replied.

"Oh, I know," Morgan answered, licking his lips, "That's why I bought us two extra onion ring orders to share."

"You did! Thanks Jerry!" we all said at the same time.

"Yer' welcome. I've got more than enough money to last me the week so I figured why not," Morgan replied. "We all earned a little something extra after that hike from hell."

"You know," Driscoll said, "That might have been one heck of a climb up to Blanca but I think it was still worth it."

"Oh! No doubt because I had some major revelations up there on that acid."

"We noticed you were kind of spaced-out in your own little world for a while," Reno remarked, glancing at me.

"You did, huh?"

"Oh, yeah. We tried talking to ya' a few times. But man, talk about out there," he said, rolling his eyes. "Especially when you were staring at those wild flowers."

"Oh really, O'Riley?"

"Yep. You sure were," and then Steve began to sing in a light hearted way, *"One sip of wine, and two sips of gin,* oh, I mean acid, *and he's lost in the ozone again."*

"Yeah, okay Reno, or should I say, Chief Flaming Lips!" And we all shared another laugh.

"So, was I the only one up there hallucinating? Cause I watched that waterfall turn into falling diamonds and the lake change colors and those wildflowers grow!" I said. After a pause Reno spoke up.

"Wish I would have seen stuff like that."

"Nothin' here," Jerry answered, shaking his head. But Driscoll didn't say anything so the three of us slowly turned our heads and stared at him.

"Okay, alright, lemme fess up," Driscoll said, the same Cheshire grin forming on his lips as the day before. "I have to admit, Bobby's half of that blotter was a little darker than mine, or the others. And, maybe, a touch bigger." I jerked my head around and looked at him, then smiled and said.

"Thanks man, loved every minute of it. You should get some more and we'll do another hike before the weather turns."

"No more hikes for me, but I'll do some more of that blotter," Jerry said.

"Acid yes, hikes no," Reno grunted. Driscoll looked at me, nodded, and then mentioned.

"My neighbor told me that over in the Olympics you can smell the salt of the sea up at Hurricane Ridge."

"No kidding. Well, I'm up for another hike anytime you are. We should check it out!" I replied.

"Cool," Driscoll answered, "and maybe do some planning."

"Better gear would help, a tent would be good. Maybe some bug spray," I offered.

"And a first-aid kit," he added, glancing down at his scarred finger.

We went back to people watching and I spied a young couple with two toddlers, a boy and girl, sitting near us having their meal. The couple looked to be in their late twenties — the kids were well-mannered and quiet.

I glanced around at all the other tourists and families and got lost in a trance. Thoughts raced through my mind about who they were, where they lived and what their lives were like. Then I told myself that I needed to figure out how to live my life and quickly realized that the most important thing I wanted in life was to be happy. Then I came to the positive conclusion that every life-changing event we experience, no matter who we are, has its own inner meaning to help shape and mold us for the future days ahead.

The thought complete — I turned back and gazed at the young family near us again and wondered if the four of us would ever have families of our own someday and if we'd even get to grow old and watch our children have families of their own. That is, because so much depended on the life of our planet. I flashed on the realization that everything in life depended on how we treated and loved each other and how the human race treated the earth. I thought about my own parents and everything they'd done and sacrificed for me and my siblings. I reminded myself how great they were, even though we hadn't been getting along the last couple of years, and told myself that I needed to stop testing them so much. So I made a personal promise to try and improve our relationship and do something for them, like maybe take them out to dinner. All of a sudden our number was called and Jerry leapt to his feet.

"That's us," he said, running off to the pick-up window.

We dove into the food and I can't tell you how good those cheeseburgers and onion rings tasted. To this day the four of us should thank our lucky stars that we didn't go off-course or get badly hurt in the wilderness that life-lesson lost weekend when we could barely find our way or feed ourselves.

MUSIC SWEET MUSIC

For want of life with music
For love of mystic song

John Prine

The lamps have all dimmed
In Muhlenberg County
There's no more John Prine
To sing us goodnight

But the songs never died
On the day April 7
We still have his anthems
To make it seem right

Sweet Revenge on the tongue
Of all that remember
When they first had
An Illegal Smile

Barbara Lewis Mr. Peabody
Sam Stone and Dear Abby
The Tree of Forgiveness
Will never grow old

John's ashes and music
Now float the Green River
Through Muhlenberg County
With the coal and our dreams

On the Mississippi and down to
The city New Orleans
And with it our love
For his Fiona and sons

Sing with me now
Sing for the poet
Sing for the man
Who brought forth the songs

Sing to remember
Sing to his memory
Sing for the time
John sang for us all

Praise be to Paradise
Donald and Lydia
Praise for the Angel
From Montgomery now flown

April 14, 2020

THE METAMORPHOSIS OF BOB WEIR

Ratdog: Moore Theater Seattle 2-17-07

I was lost in a sunshine daydream, driving from Chelan County and stuck in a slow moving line of cars on Stevens Pass, when a Red-tailed hawk suddenly appeared next to me flying at forty miles an hour. Right as I noticed him it glanced at me, vigorously flapped its wings, cut across my windshield and then flew over towards the Baring house, east of Everett in the Cascades that my old cohorts Vic and Anna used to live in.

"I've just been blessed," I said to myself, and watched as the hawk flew right at the tiny one bedroom home where I had so many past memories. *"Was that hawk trying to communicate with me?"*

Steve O'Riley, Mike Bolt and I had tickets for a Bob Weir show with his band Ratdog at the Moore Theatre that night and I for one had not been to the Moore for over 30 years to see a show. Once I arrived in Port Gardner at O'Riley's house I found Bolt was already there. We all agreed that none of us had been to the theatre since we'd seen the Jerry Garcia Band there in 1976, 31 years before. For the past 12 years since Jerry had died we'd been lucky to have RatDog coming around on tour fulfilling our musical needs but never at the Moore.

In Seattle we casually strolled to the venue and quickly found that a line of a hundred or so like-minded tie-dyed wearing people had already formed. The minute we got to the back of the line we were approached by a street person who had something to say. He told us all about how he was currently working with drug addicted homeless kids and selling candy bars that he claimed were donated to him to help support this program. As we listened, along with the others in line, another vendor of a different sort approached and stepped between us and the candy salesman and asked Reno if he'd like to buy some, "Jolly Vegetables."

Reno immediately entered into a transactional conversation with the new vendor and cut a deal to buy some shrooms. It offended the candy seller and he started in on the "Vegetable Salesman."

"Hey man, that's not cool," the Candyman said.

"Well, hey mister, I don't want to fight with you." Back and forth they went then separated and left.

"Wow," Reno observed, "That was the classic confrontation of the Angel and the Devil. First the Angel shows up and then the Devil comes in right behind."

"It's the Ying and the Yang," I said.

"The Good and the Evil," Bolt replied.

Between the Hawk up on Alpine Pass and the Angel / Devil Confrontation I knew right then that this was not going to be your run of the mill, average, go-to-a-concert-in-Seattle night. Once inside, past memories of the Moore Theatre returned, the 100 year old hall had high ceilings, chandeliers and double balconies with ornate touches of days long past. We had tickets for the main floor and got right down front, about 7 rows back from the stage. As we took in the scene we chatted about old times and said hello to the other concert goers around us. I always enjoyed looking at all the gear on stage beforehand and tonight I spied a pedal steel guitar. *"Maybe we're going to have a guest appearance?"*

The lights go down and the band comes out. Bobby ambled on wearing brown khakis, sandals, and a blue t-shirt but with his unkept mane of stubbly Einstein like hair, bushy grey beard and more lines on his face than the gig two years before at the Showbox, he kinda looked like a mad musical-scientist.

They began like always with a short jam, which this time was kicked off by drummer Jay Lane. It was a funky groove that moved along nicely until Weir and lead guitar player Mark Karan struck the opening power chord of Shakedown Street and the whole place leapt to their feet for the Garcia classic. The place was packed and the aisles were instantly filled with twirlers. As I smelled the first bit of 'Substance,' I said to myself, *"God I love the smell of pot in a public place."* It was a total and complete flash back, it's the 70s all over again. Bobby's on stage, the band was hot, the twirlers were twirling and the smell of victory was in the air.

The tightness of those guys amazed me. They'd been playing now for a good number of years with Jay Lane being the longest member since 1996. In 1998 Jeff Chimenti played his first RatDog show, then Mark Karan joined sometime around 1999 right after the first incarnation of The Others Ones was formed.

Saxophonist Kenny Brooks joined up in 2000 and bass player Robin Sylvester was the most recent member joining in 2003. It was very clear that this group of musicians loved playing together; noticeable by the visible smiles on their faces, positive body language and soaring energy.

During the appropriate chorus in Shakedown of "Don't tell me this town ain't got no heart / you just gotta poke around," I found myself nodding in agreement. Then Weir eased the band into, It's All Over Now, Baby Blue, a Dylan song that Jerry covered regularly in the Dead. After the first few verses Jeff Chimenti treated us to a fine piano solo and then Mark Karan took the reins and played a wonderful guitar passage. Bob stepped back to the microphone and sang, "Strike another match, go start anew / cause it's all over now, baby blue," I swear it felt like he was singing just for me. I felt a real connection right there, it reconfirmed my belief in RatDog and the whole Grateful Dead family which the three of us had been a devoted part of since 1970.

After coming to a close on Baby Blue, Weir did a quick countdown into Ramble on Rose and it was just starting to become apparent that he was in the beginning throws of a Garcia infused night. Then Weir played the melodic entry into Friend of the Devil and it was apparent that Bob had the spirit of Jerry inside of him on this particular night in Seattle.

Next we got a new song, Tuesday Blues, a mid-tempo funky rhythm backed with the chorus of, "Tuesday Blues had 'em all week long / goin' round and round." Towards the end of the song Mark Karan fingered the opening riff of Last Time by The Rolling Stones. What a great nod to the Rock n' Roll Legend and Legacy of Keith Richards! Everyone in the band was singing all the verses and it was obvious that they were having a grand old time. The crowd was loving it and the group was too. They were rocking along and I thought to myself that this might be the last song in the first set, but no. At the end of it, the guitars stayed on and they slid into another new song, She Says, a slow number with a distinct Deadlike groove. Weir topped off this new one with yet another Garcia song, Liberty. Talk about paying respects! It seemed so far like the whole night had been a Garcia tribute. By the time he got to the chorus, "Ooo Freedom / Ooo Liberty / I'm gonna find my own way home," the whole place was singing along and my spine was tingling. This combined with "The Smell of Victory in the Air," made me feel so proud to be part of the celebration that waves of elation spread through me. I told myself that this had to be the last song of the set when they went straight into Eyes of the World.

Eyes, which any fundamentalist Dead Head will tell you was one of Garcia's favorite Jam Songs of all time and Bandleader Bob built it slowly with the opening line, "Right outside this lazy summer home," and the whole crowd was right with him. After the first verse the jam was a comfort groove that Mark Karan carried to a higher intensity. Weir stepped back to the microphone and sang, "There comes a redeemer, and he slowly too fades away," and I knew I was in the Church of Jerry Garcia having fellowship. "And there follows his wagon behind him that's loaded with clay," was his following passage and I'm seeing him as the morphed deity of Jerry. I'm staring at musical mad-scientist Bob and sure enough he's Jerry! Bushy white beard with his longer than normal uncombed

Einstein grey mane and it became apparent to me that gone were the days of him with the preppy look and blow dry hair, "Holy Moses Bobby has morphed into Jerry! But without the weight!" On a granular level I was instantly bathed in the eternal spirit of Garcia, waves of primordial rapture moved through my body.

RatDog meanwhile had transported the packed house of 1,800 devout followers into a jam so powerful, so connected that at the crescendo I saw the look of amazement on Weir's face as he was watching Kenny Brooks blow the most incredible series of notes out of his horn. It appeared that he was being transported into a world of total admiration, as much as we were. And as quickly as it had started, with a quick wave of his hand Bob brings to a close the first set. He announced a quick break and we all looked at each other with blissful smiles.

We rave about what we've just witnessed and comment about how in the hell he was gonna top the first set. And Bolt in his infinite wisdom said, "Now Bobby's the man, he'll top it."

"Sounds good to me," Reno added. After a trip to an overly-packed restroom we settled in for a highly anticipated second set and commented about who was going to sit down at the pedal steel.

Thirty minutes later they came back on and, sure enough, a rather distinguished looking, dapperly dressed gentleman sat down at the work-bench-like instrument. Weir usually started his second set's acoustic and this show was no different. He and the steel player talked over a few things and then Bob picked out the intro of Jack-A-Roe, a traditional folksong. With the strains of the new pedal player, Robin on stand-up bass and Karan also on acoustic guitar, Weir sang the story of the sea captain and his bride to be. For years Jerry covered this old time sea shanty, both acoustic and electric, and now Bobby has taken it under his wing. At the instrumental break the pedal player did a very Jerry-esque lead passage and at the end Weir offered a quick introduction, "Ed Littlefield," and the crowd raved in approval. As soon as he said, "Ed Littlefield," I recognized the name right away. The previous Seattle show at the Showbox,

Bob had a guest mandolin player, Danny Wheetman, and I did some research. I found him to be a member of a group by the name of Marley's Ghost and got their latest CD, Spooked. I also learned that Mr. Littlefield had been a member of that band too and a past member of the greater Seattle area troubadours, Lance Romance and the 3 Minute Boogie in the 1970s. Plus some of Marley's Ghost made their home in Snohomish County. *"What a special treat,"* I thought to myself, and local Arlington friends at that.

At the end of Jack-A-Roe, he once again mentioned Ed's name and then proceeded to introduce the next song as a Buck Owens number titled A-11 featuring the "weeping strains of Ed Littlefield." Bob then went on to make the statement, "Cheaters never prosper." Which I guessed had to do with the story line of the song, and soon learned were the call letters to a lonesome tune on the jukebox in a small town where there was apparently a little extra-marital shenanigans going on. Once again during the instrumental break Ed played the most comfortable and correct lead passage on his pedal steel that melded splendidly in the song. Absolute perfection.

As the Buck Owens number began to fade Bob went into the beginning chord changes to The Weight by The Band, and the crowd immediately recognized it. The place went nuts for this classic of all time songs. By the time Weir got to the second verse of, "I picked up my bag, I went lookin' for a place to hide / When I saw Carmen and the Devil walkin' side by side," it all became clear to me. He was painting an overarching depiction of Jerry and the times they shared in the form of a musical masterpiece. The verse of Carmen and the Devil, with our own visit with the Devil and the Angel before the show, the Hawk on Stevens Pass, plus with the Metamorphosis of Bob into Jerry Revelation I was lifted into a place of supreme being. I once again reminded myself about taking fellowship in the Church of Jerry Garcia and everything in the world was right. With Ed Littlefield adding just the right color to the painting, at just the right time, all of the notes were tinted with the right touches creating a Garcia Musical Collage.

With what sounded like a rehearsed ending to The Weight, the song ended and Ed, our new favorite pedal steel player, left the stage while Jeff Chimenti signaled the mellow and haunting keyboard intro of Lost Sailor, and finally Bobby began his first somewhat vintage original song after over two hours into the show! But when he sang, "Where's the Dark Star," once again Jerry came to mind in this Garcia Painting evening. When he sang, "There's a price for being free," I was set off once again to another world and related back to the earlier chorus of, "Ooo Freedom." It seemed like Weir was connecting the dots to the night's masterpiece and brought it all together into one musical family night of cosmic travels.

The Lost Sailor jam pushed the band into the segue which became, Saint of Circumstance. A rockin' favorite which always followed Sailor and started with the refrain "This Must Be Heaven," which on this night of fellowship seemed so apropos.

Behind Bob drummer Jay Lane was a driving machine, pounding, pushing, moving the beat and band along with a power so huge it felt like he was going to launch us all into a new hemisphere. He appeared to be the pulse of the group when all of a sudden Weir gave a wave of his hand and brought the jam to a crashing end only to signal the entry into He's Gone, the Hunter - Garcia song written thirty-five years prior about the firing of the Grateful Dead's manager at that time, Lenny Hart, a song which a year after its composition had become a heartfelt goodbye to band member Ron "Pigpen" McKernan in 1973, was now a benediction to Jerry Garcia.

Bobby and Jay Lane sang the chorus of, "Like I told Ya / What I said / Steal your face right off your head," the whole crowd sang along and continued right into, "Now he's gone / Lord he's gone / Like a steam Locomotive / Rolling down the tracks," I felt like I was at a Jerry Garcia Wake and revival. Once again Mark Karan signaled the instrumental break and I sensed his guitar playing was building that railroad track for Jerry's Steam Locomotive, tie by tie, rail by rail. Until Weir stepped back up and returned to the "Like I Told Ya," segment and then slowed it down and turned the song into an a-Capella "Old Time Religious Resurrection" with all the members harmonizing. I felt like I'd been fully baptized and confirmed in the Church of Garcia & Weir. He brought it down to a hush and then sounded out the notes for the Jam to follow and took us all home. The jam started in the He's Gone vein and then twisted and turned into The Other One. Fantastic! I could feel the space/drums segment of the show coming and Weir retreated from the stage.

The rest of the players slowly brought the jam down to where it was just Jay Lane going into what we thought was the always present second set drum solo when he announced, "I want to bring out my homie." To our surprise from the darkness of back stage came a young man carrying a set of — bagpipes! He strode to front center stage, blew into the pipes, and began a fast Irish Jig. To which Jay Lane backed him with a very appropriate beat. Two seconds into this new and never heard of musical display my jaw dropped and I was absolutely astounded. The whole place was on their feet screaming and enjoying a treat of all treats. Bagpipe guy and Jay Lane started building the song and then Robin on bass came back and added color to "The Jig" and then Jeff Chimenti chimed in on the piano. Everyone in the theater was completely entranced by this display of unannounced, unbelievable, musical improvisation. They go and go for 3 or 4 minutes and the entire place was dancing an Irish Jig and just as quickly as it started it ended while the whole place was screaming with delight. The roar of the crowd was overwhelming and Mr. Bagpipes took off his instrument and raised it over his head in a sort of salute, the applause became deafening. Total Elation! Once the crowd quieted down Weir came back on stage with Ed Littlefield and signaled Mr. Bagpipes to stay and began Wharf Rat, and I told myself, *"Jerry Lives!"*

With the bagpipes bringing an eerie backdrop to the song Bobby completed his portrait of Garcia. Using the song as the ultimate compliment to Jerry, he had his painting of Garcia finished, framed, and hung on the theater wall. Wharf Rat was first introduced to us on the Skull & Roses album in 1971 and as young kids growing up on Port Gardner Bay that particular album was our, 'Anthem to Existence.' The power of the song was brought to a new level with the 8 musicians on stage. Weir had them firing on all cylinders and after getting through the first few verses he came to, "I Got a Girl / Named Bonnie Lee / I Know That Girl's Been True To Me," and the whole place was in the palm of his hand. They climbed and climbed to the top of a lofty peak with the sound of distant bagpipes urging them on. Higher and higher they went when all of a sudden on the turn of a dime he redirected the members into the next song.

Just like that the band has completely reversed direction and Weir quickly introduces "Jori Chisholm" on bagpipes, and Jori raised his bagpipes once again then exited the stage as Weir and Crew tore into One More Saturday Night.

Seeing how it actually was a Saturday night I was sure that Bob just couldn't help but dust off his old favorite. He sang, "The President come on the news / Says I get no satisfaction / That's why I sing the blues," and then mentioned the name George (Bush) in the next line and I said to myself that the night was now complete. The band was rockin', the place was hopin', and it sounded and looked like the Moore was gonna burst. It was pandemonium when he screamed, "Playin' on a Saturday Night," and it felt like we'd reached lift off. We finally got to the big crashing ending, they stepped off stage, the house lights stayed off and we cheered and cheered until they finally returned for an encore.

RatDog plugged back in, Weir counted down and they broke into US Blues, Hunter and Garcia's official anthem of life in the USA. "Red and White / Blue Suede Shoes / I'm Uncle Sam / How Do You Do." At the chorus of, "Wave That Flag" a very tall, long-bearded older hippie came out from backstage and walked back and forth behind the group's amplifiers with an American flag held high that had a white peace sign in the blue field. Everybody went nuts and this guy was waving the flag high and proud as hell! We are all flipping out and at the end of the chorus he darted out of sight. After another rousing verse the Peace Flag Guy was back during the "Wave That Flag" chorus and this time he walked back and forth between the group members and Bobby and then darted back off stage. Bob sang the final verse "Summertime / Come and Gone /

My Oh My," then went into the chorus and once again Peace Man returned but this last time he was right out in front of Weir at center stage walking and waving his flag and we were all dam near saluting this wonderful display of hippie patriotism. What a fitting end to an absolutely wonderful evening.

At the song's end Weir reintroduced Ed and Jori and everyone lined up, including Peace Guy with his flag, at the front of the stage for a bow before a most appreciative audience. We all waved goodbye and watched as they left. As we filed out of the venue we couldn't help but rave about the evening's event.

"Best RatDog show ever" I said, smiling.

"No kiddin'," Bolt replied.

"That Eyes of the World was something else, wasn't it?" Reno offered.

"Yep, and what about Wharf Rat! With those bagpipes!" I added.

"Loved it," Bolt said. "Wharf Rat was the song that made me a Dead Head."

"Really?" Reno said, looking at Mike. "I didn't know that. Althea's always been my favorite, but Bob sure had the spirit of Jerry in him tonight," Reno said.

"That's exactly what I was thinking the whole show!" I replied.

Once back at the car we cracked open a few beers and toasted the night and ourselves under the stars standing in an empty parking lot. The city was quiet and it seemed like everything was at peace in the world. The Metamorphosis of Bob Weir, in my mind, was complete and it was almost too good to be true, because the work and art of Jerry Garcia was still alive and bound to live in eternity.

Someone once said, "All good things must end," and a Prankster will tell you, "Nothing lasts." I guess whoever came up with those statements was right and on that night we did not want it to end, but we really had no choice, or did we?

Once we were back on the freeway headed north, surrounded by all the fast moving cars, the cold hard fact of coming back to reality set in. For the last few hours we had been happy travelers on a road built by Bob and his band so coming back to the real world was just not quite where we wanted to be yet, at least not for me. We knew that the next Bobby show was scheduled for Vancouver, BC right up the road and seeing how we were headed that way it just seemed natural to drive right on by the rest of the world and keep on, *"Truckin'."*

RAVING ON THE GODFATHER
OF SOUTHERN ROCK

Dickey Betts & Great Southern Copper Mountain, Colorado

At Copper Mountain's Guitar Town Music Festival, Dickey Betts and his thirty year old son Duane brought their very special brand of Southern Rock to the top of the Rocky Mountains with their band Great Southern. For the closing slot of the two-day July 2007 music festival Dickey led his six piece band onto a portable base-area stage jam-packed with a double stack of Marshall Amplifiers and a string of Gibson guitars. A crowd of a few thousand greeted them with the rousing sound of welcoming applause.

Dressed in his signature western garb of straw cowboy hat with feathers, denim shirt, jeans and alligator boots, Dickey strapped on his Les Paul Sunburst and counted off the beginnings to the power instrumental Les Brers in A Minor, signaling to the Mountain Gods and all present that he was there to make a musical statement. With a determined look on his face, he plowed through the challenging piece of music and made it very well known right off that he deserved his rightful place at the altar of Southern Rock-N-Roll. Dickey and his son Duane turned this already powerful song into a monster opener and left everyone at Copper slack jawed and amazed. What a way to say, "Hello Rocky Mountains."

After a good fifteen minutes the opener was over and Dickey turned to his two drummers and counted them off into Statesboro Blues. Hammond B-3 Organ player Mike Kach tackled the vocals and did an excellent job with twinges of Greg Allman in his voice. During the solo break Dickey and Duane went into a call and respond dueling guitars segment that left us all screaming for more.

Finally, on the third song, Betts stepped up to the microphone and we got, Change My Way of Living, from the Great Southern release, The Collectors, his song about cleaning up and getting straight. The band's on fire right out of the gate and it was clear that they were all happy to be high in the Rockies.

When he stepped back to the mic we got Blue Sky and his voice was clear and crisp with just a touch of age for good measure. Dickey recorded Blue Sky with his historic band mate of old, Duane Allman, just before Duane's tragic motorcycle accident in late 1971. Talk about a good feeling when he sang, "You're my Blue Sky / You're my Sunny Day / Lord You Know You Make Me High When You Turn Your Love My Way," and they flew into that wonderful slide guitar statement.

Then BOOM! The bass player, Pedro Arevalo, pounded out the beginning low end notes to Hoochie Coochie Man, and Dickey and Crew launched us all into the stratosphere! Pedro Arevalo's bass playing was flat out unbelievable. Wearing a wide brimmed hat, reminiscent of Butch Trucks back in the original Allman Brothers days, and with thick black dreadlocks weighing down his back, Pedro stepped to the microphone and told us, "I'll Be Your Hoochie Coochie Man / I'll Set You Free!" The two drummers were pounding out the beat and the three guitar army of Dickey, Duane and Andy Aledort were machine gunning their Marshall Amplified Sound into the peaks of the Rocky Mountains.

They finally came to a crashing close and Dickey began to pick out the beginning notes of One Way Out. When Duane (named after Duane Allman) came in on his Goldtop Les Paul with the exact Duane Allman slide part I was fully transcended back in time to when the Allman Brothers ruled the Rock-n-Roll World. Organ player Mike Kach nailed the vocal, the drummers went into a short pounding solo, much like the studio version, and then Zing, off they fly into guitar army time with all three playing their hearts out. And during this multi-jam I noticed that all players were directly wired to their amps. No wireless connections for Great Southern, no newfangled high-tech contraptions for this hard working band, they were all wired for sound into their stack of Marshall Amps and I am loving them for it! It's like I'm listening to Dickey Kilowatt and the Great Megawatt Southern. The power that those guys were putting out was collapsing my chest for Christ Sakes! Fan Flippin' Tastic! During the guitar break I could see Duane keeping a constant watchful eye on his father. I sensed a real connection between father and son as they played back and forth, to and against each other.

As One Way Out faded Dickey led the band right into In Memory of Elizabeth Reed, his milestone instrumental. The song went up and down, back and forth, through many changes and movements. The poly-rhythms of the drummers was mesmerizing and extremely tight, flowing and very precise. On and on Elizabeth Reed sojourns, Betts kept challenging his son to take the song farther and higher, on and on they go, it just kept building and building. I was floored at how Dickey challenged Duane in a guitar battle as they played back and forth. Then he went toe to toe with the bass player and they whipped the song into a frenzy. Finally he brought it all down and signaled the drum break.

Dickey took off his guitar and gestured for the always present drum solo and a quick break for the rest of the group. The drummers took turns, first Frankie Lombardi, and then James Varnado, to give each other a break. I could see behind the drum risers Betts sitting on a cooler and enjoying a cold one. He was going to turn 64 this year and was as energetic as ever and looking very good for what I was coming to realize, that Dickey Betts "is" The Godfather of Southern Rock.

After the drum segment the members strolled back on stage and went right back into Elizabeth Reed again. They picked up right where they left off and now they took Elizabeth to the outer limits. Dickey just seemed to have some leftover business with the song and wanted to make it very clear to all of us that In Memory of Elizabeth Reed was his signature piece, his shinning statement, his Rosetta Stone.

They brought us all back to earth when Betts stepped to the mic and they turned a sharp corner into 7 Turns, the titular song from the great Allman Brothers 1990 record of the same name. When he sang, "Somebody's Callin' Your Name / Somebody's Waitin' for You," the biggest chill ran up my spine. It was like he was calling out to everyone there. *"What a great rock-n-roll moment, what pure and perfect American music,"* I said to myself. During the guitar break Dickey and Duane were smiling at each other, looking really happy, dodging each other to make room on stage, playing to the crowd and the roadies off stage, just flat out having the time of their lives while they did call and respond on and on through the song as dusk began to come over Copper Mountain.

Once 7 Turns ended Betts turned to adjust his amplifier controls, got it right, spun on his boot heel back to the crowd and then kicked off the opening riff of Back Where It All Begins, the calypso influenced poly rhythm song that he wrote in 1994 from the last good Allman Brothers studio album. And right then and there I came to the realization that Dickey Betts and Great Southern were out Allman-ing the Allman Brothers. His determined look when he first hit the stage now brought me to the full understanding that he had something to prove and they were damn well proving it! Betts deserves to wear the Crown of the King of Southern Rock, and he has earned it! As he played a solo with his eyes closed, the beginning to be seen stars shimmered above forming a perfect sky ceiling for the song. Then he opened his eyes wide and stepped back to the mic and sang the final verse, and took the band into a Mountain Jam type ending to close out the number.

And without hesitation Dickey strapped on a Fender Stratocaster and launched the band into No One to Run With, with the Not Fade Away drum beat intro, organ player Mike Kach once again tackled the vocal and killed it with his grisly delivery right before Dickey and the Great Southern guitar army took over and pushed everyone to the outer limits of our Rocky Mountain evening. I couldn't help but remember how Greg Allman had ushered Betts out of the Allman Brothers in 2000. Back when Duane Allman passed away in 1971, Dickey single handedly picked up the torch and more than filled in for his fallen band mate and friend. It was Dickey Betts who kept the Allman Brothers on the Rock-n-Roll Map after Duane's accident and then he did it again when original bass player Barry Oakley died in a similar accident less than a year later. He was the one that kept the hits coming back in those years and deserves his rightful place in the history of Southern Rock and his rightful place, back in The Allman Brothers.

Signaling the close of Run With, Dickey counted off to the keyboard player and kicked off Jessica, his classic instrumental released right after Barry Oakley's death and dedicated to him. And while we are paying our rightful respects to Mr. Betts it should be remembered that he wrote over half of the Brothers and Sisters albums songs, once again proving the profound importance of his continuing legacy! During Jessica, he led the band on and on, higher and higher, signaling Duane to take the lead, and then into a piano break that built and built until it sounded like they were going to flat out explode. They continued higher and farther to where Dickey finally hit the power chord to the songs end only to extend the ending with more chords up and down the neck of his guitar and just when I thought it was over he took them into another round of closing chords and kept extending and extending it. I was thinking, this is the longest, most powerful ending statement in the History of Rock. The crowd was going nuts, Great Southern was still putting the finishing touches on the longest ending of any live song that I've ever heard, and then with a series of guitar army booms, the song came to a crashing crescendo finality! "Holy Mother of All Rock Show Endings!"

Off the stage they went with the crowd screaming for more. I said to myself, *"I bet he comes back and closes with Ramblin' Man."* And sure enough, he strolled back on stage and played it. I remembered the determined look on Dickey's face at the beginning of the show and realized that his performance was a statement to the world that he wasn't going anywhere.

And as I watched Dickey and his bandmates finish the encore and finally exit the stage for the night a lightning bolt like feeling hit me and took me back in time to all the music of the '60s and '70s that influenced me so much, those songs instantly pumped through my heart and welled up in my chest in a memorable tapestry. I recalled being mesmerized by Bob Dylan's seminal hit Like a Rolling Stone on a neighbor's transistor radio out on the sidewalk in the summer of 1965, to the first time I heard the painful refrain of Janis Joplin belting out Piece of My Heart, The Byrds' jangling rhythms of Mr. Tambourine Man, the scorching hard rock of Led Zeppelin II, Let It Bleed's stark reality, the vivid storytelling on Grateful Dead's Workingman's Dead, Neil Young's lyrical import of After the Gold Rush, the postmortem masterfulness of Gram Parsons' Grievous Angel, to the otherworldly brilliance of Gene Clark's No Other and on and on and on. And all I could think was, "Thank you Dickey Betts and Great Southern. Thank you for the music and contributing to the continuing culture of our times."

DEDICATION

Without art, and lifelong friendships,
man's quest would be incomplete

Travelin' Reno Blues

Variations on a theme
Nuance to the bone
Heaven's giant sneeze
He rules Cajolery's Throne

Zen of magnetism
Embellishment in tune
The stuntman turns cartwheels
In the shadows of the moon

Whimsy wit and wisdom
Have left us much too soon
An empty bottle — trade a word
For the Travelin' Reno Blues

Variations on a life
Variations come in threes
One for loss and sorrow
Two for the widow's plea

There's a turning in the river
Slack water in the tide
No one can replace
The one who was my guide

But the Traveling Reno Blues
Are all we're left to use
A good man rocks
A great man sings — The Travelin' Reno Blues

Jan. 2009

Indian Prayer
Chief Yellow Lark, Lakota

Oh, Great Spirit, whose voice I hear in the winds.
And whose breath gives life to all the world.
Hear me! I am small and weak.
I need your strength and wisdom.
Let me walk in beauty, and make my eyes
Ever hold the red and purple sunset.
Make my hands respect the things you have made.
My ear sharp to hear your voice.
Make me wise so that I may understand
The things you might teach me.
Let me learn the lessons you have hidden
In every leaf and rock.
I seek strength, not to be greater than my brother.
But to fight my greatest enemy, myself.
Make me always ready to come to you
With clear hands and straight eyes.
So when life fades, as the fading sunset.
My spirit may come to you without shame.

THE GREAT WHITE BUFFALO'S
FINAL STATEMENT

The sky was clear, the air was cold and still. The afternoon sun gleamed off the snow pack of the Cascade peaks on the horizon, but cloudy thoughts cluttered my mind; I still had not reached full closure with the overwhelming loss of my dear old friend Steve "Reno" Rowley, just one week before.

I was parked beside an orchard, surrounded by leafless pear trees on a deserted county road northwest of Cashmere. My window was open and there were a few crows in the orchard, cackling back and forth to each other. It sounded as if they were having a conversation and the longer I listened to them the more I felt privileged to be eavesdropping on their personal discussions.

As the crows debated I tried to enjoy a cigar while thinking about Reno, recalling some of the times we had spent growing up. When out of nowhere a string of dangling, multi-colored yarn appeared, hanging mid-air right next to me for some inexplicable reason. I was stunned and taken aback! How on earth had it gotten here, let alone come to end up next to me? I stuck my head out the window and looked up. A red balloon hovered ten feet off the ground, five feet from my driver side door. I felt an inexpressible sense of wonder as it lingered, motionless. I couldn't take my eyes away from it, let alone blink, instantly it had my full undivided attention.

Thirty seconds later the balloon began moving ever so slowly, even though there wasn't a lick of wind, and turned in front of the windshield. It passed directly in front of me, crossed the road and rose up ten more feet. In doing so the balloon floated just above the bare trees of the orchard across the way, and then dropped down into some of them. It stopped between four sets of limbs that formed a sort of picture frame from my angle and stayed there suspended for minutes as I stared at it, entranced. Time seemed to stand still. I waited and wondered if this occurrence had some kind of otherworldly meaning.

Then I flashed on the supernatural and wondered if Steve had his finger on that balloon and guided it to me from heaven above, like a message, saying, "Hey, it's all right. I'm okay. Go on with your life. I'll see you again, don't worry."

After a few moments it began to shudder from side to side, as if to wave, and at that point I knew there was no doubt, it was Reno, up on high, giving me a celestial sign, a kind of extrasensory acknowledgment. As I stared, it seemed to be staring back. Then I figured it out — the colorful yarn hanging from it was his final embellished story, his last statement, his final tall tale of yarn to spin into lint.

Then it rose, the yarn untangled, not snagged or the balloon popped by the jagged outreached pear tree limbs and hovered just above the orchard! Slowly, it began to climb. I stayed fixated upon its lofty path as it turned and set on a dead reckoning path of true north, until it had gained enough altitude to pass over the lone pine studded ridge high above and I said, "Thank you Great White Buffalo. Thank you for releasing me. Thank you Steve for your unwavering friendship. I'll see you again someday."

Closure
Amen
Winter 2009

CODA

Life's curvy road only ends with a new path

Paper Highway

Come ride with me
On the Paper Highway
Where dreams can be found
Find A New Kind of Yesterday

No stop signs there'll be
Red lights 'er street scenes
Just the freedom to drive
Get away from everything

The stories we'd tell
Tall tales an' remedies
The sights and the sounds
Rolling ecstasy

Deserts and valleys
Mountains and streams
And everything else
We passed in between

This life and the next
The Great Beyond
Love and Mercy
Might be in the next town

Follow your Heart
Down the Paper Highway
Exalted traveling
On free-spirit by-ways

Radio station
Convertible down
Changing the channel
To a rock-n-roll sound

Roadside Attractions
Great Notions are few
There's no Satisfaction
Only Led Zeppelin II

Desert land ghost towns
Billboards and sand
Vultures and cactus
Prairie dog mounds

Bound for the Crossroads
There's no turning back
On The Road (in the glove box)
by Jack Kerouac

The Teachings of Castaneda
And Fear and Loathing
They all Come Together
East of Eden

Gas station cigarettes
Cold beer on ice
Road map cheap motels
Café's dinettes

Stay in the lane
Don't cross the white line
But cross all those t's
And dot all those i's

Words upon words
Adjectives an' nouns
Verbs roll by swift
When a story has to be found

No need to worry
When you slip outta town
You'll be paying the fiddler
Once you come back around

Plenty of ink
On the Paper Highway
Letters and vowels
The last sentence complete

Enough has been said
Even more written down
Thank you for coming
I'll meet you uptown

I hope you've enjoyed
The path this tome's taken
It's gone by so fast
Fifty years in the makin'

"What a long strange trip it's been!"

2020

ACKNOWLEDGMENTS

At this time I'd like to sincerely thank my favorite person in the world, Susan Harrell, for being a wonderful counselor, spiritual advisor, editor, proofreader and best friend. I want to also sincerely thank my son Skyler Cuthill who eagerly served as my faithful editor. I could not have completed this publication without their work, help and support.

I'm dedicating Paper Highway to my astute colleague and dearly departed friend Steve Rowley to show my appreciation of him for being the first to encourage me to share my poetry and writing; I will forever be indebted to Steve. Thank you Reno for providing the extra encouragement I needed to act upon my dreams.

I'd like to give credit to my creative writing teacher at Everett High School, Irene Brantner, for instilling in me the love of words, language and ideas. I will always remember the day when she said, "There are no rules in poetry." I liked the sound of that.

I am thankful to all of the following for the love, motivation and support they've shown over the years throughout my many projects: my daughter Cassidy, parents Jim & Jeanne, sister Diane and her husband Terry, brother Dave and his wife Marikay, cousin MC and her husband Gunter, Mike & Nancy Oshie, Miles & Jill Auckland, Bill & Karen Jamieson, Pete & Bonnie Frothingham, Jim Parker, Jim Agnew, Gary Morrill, Mike & Jill Johnson, Jacqueline Cruver, Dian Rowley Frothingham for providing the photo of Steve, the Rowley Family and the extended Gopher Broke Family

Love you all.

ABOUT THE AUTHOR

Malstrom Award winning author J.D. Howard was born at West Seattle, raised at Everett, Washington and graduated from EHS in 1973. He currently lives in the foothills of Snohomish County and is the proud father of two children. Other works include: The Pride of Monte Cristo (2019) Sawdust Empire (2016) and Both Sides of The Wish (2013).

CHAPTER SYMBOL KEY

Whimsy = Chaos Magic Symbol: A contemporary magic that was based on the philosophies of Austin Osman Spare (1886-1956) and initially developed in England in the 1970s. Sometimes referred to as success magic or results-based magic, chaos magic claims to emphasize the attainment of specific results over the symbolic, ritualistic, theological or otherwise ornamental aspects of other traditions. Chaos magicians subsequently treat belief as a tool, often creating their own idiosyncratic magical systems and frequently borrowing from other magical traditions, religious movements, popular culture and various strands of philosophy

Faith & Family = Infinity Symbol: The Infinity symbol is a mathematical concept that represents something boundless or endless or something that is larger than any real or natural number. Since the time of the ancient Greeks, the nature of infinity was the subject of many discussions among philosophers. The symbol was introduced in the 17th Century.

The Natural World = The Tree of Life: This symbol is a fundamental widespread myth or archetype in many of the world's mythologies, religious and philosophical traditions. It is closely related to the concept of the sacred tree. The tree of knowledge, connecting to heaven and the underworld, and the tree of life, connecting all forms of creation, are both forms of the world tree or cosmic tree, and are portrayed in various religions and philosophies as the same tree.

Childhood = Egyptian Ankh Symbol for Life: The Ankh is an ancient Egyptian hieroglyphic symbol that was most commonly used in writing and in Egyptian art to represent the word for life and, by extension, as a symbol of life itself. The origins of the symbol are not known, although many hypotheses have been proposed. In art the symbol often appeared as a physical object representing either life or substances such as air or water that are related to it.

War & Politics = Lady Justice: Lady Justice is an allegorical personification of the moral force in judicial systems. Her attributes are a blindfold, a balance scale, and a sword. She often appears as a pair with Prudetia, who holds a mirror and a snake. Lady Justice originates from the personification of Justice in Ancient Roman art.

North Fork = Yin Yang: In Ancient Chinese Philosophy, Yin and Yang is a concept of dualism, describing how seemingly opposite or contrary forces may actually be complementary, interconnected, and interdependent in the natural world, and how they may give rise to each other as they interrelate to one another. In Chinese cosmology, the universe creates itself out of a primary chaos of material energy, organized into the cycles of Yin and Yang and formed into objects and lives. Yin is the receptive and Yang the active principle, seen in all forms of change and difference such as the annual cycle (winter and summer), the landscape (north-facing shade and south-facing brightness), the formation of both women and men as characters (male and female coupling) and sociopolitical history (disorder and order).

Love & Mercy = Adinkra Symbol of Love: Adinkra are symbols that represent concepts and are used extensively in fabrics and pottery among the Ashantis of Ashanti Kingdom. They are incorporated into walls and other architectural features, weaved into fabric or carved on furniture for domestic and ritual use. The symbols have a decorative function but also represent objects that encapsulate evocative messages that convey traditional wisdom, aspects of life or the environment. There are many different symbols with distinct meanings, often linked with proverbs.

The Great Beyond = Celtic Cross: The Celtic Cross is a form of Christian cross featuring a nimbus or ring that emerged in Ireland, France and Britain in the Early Middle Ages. A type of ringed cross, it became widespread through its use in the stone high crosses erected across the islands, especially in regions evangelized by Irish missionaries, from the 9th through the 12th centuries. A staple of insular art, the Celtic cross is essentially a Latin cross with a nimbus surrounding the intersection of the arms and stem. Scholars have debated its exact origins, but it is related to earlier crosses featuring rings. The form gained new popularity during the Celtic Revival of the 19th century; the name "Celtic Cross" is a convention dating from that time. The shape, usually decorated with interlace and other motifs from insular art, became popular for funerary monuments and other uses.

Cosmic Commentary = Greek Eye of Horus: also known as wadjet, wedjat or udjat, is an ancient Egyptian symbol of protection and good health. The Eye of Horus is similar to the Eye of Ra, which belongs to a different god, Ra, but represents many of the same concepts. Funerary amulets were often made in the shape of the Eye of Horus. The symbol was intended to protect the pharaoh in the afterlife and to ward off evil. Ancient Egyptian and Middle-Eastern sailors would frequently paint the symbol on the bows of their vessels to ensure safe sea travel.

Music Sweet Music = Greek Lyre: The lyre is a string instrument known for its use in Greek classic antiquity and later periods. The lyre is similar in appearance to a small harp but with distinct differences. In organology, lyre is defined as a "yoke lute", being a lute in which the strings are attached to a yoke that lies in the same plane as the sound-table and consists of two arms and a cross-bar. In Ancient Greece, recitations of lyric poetry were accompanied by lyre playing.

Dedication = Celtic Tree of Life: Many types of trees found in the Celtic Nations are considered to be sacred, whether as symbols, or due to medicinal properties, or because they are seen as the abode of particular nature spirits. Historically and in folklore, the respect given to trees varies in different parts of the Celtic world.

Coda = Buddhist Ensō Symbol: In Zen Buddhism, Ensō is a sacred symbol often referred to as "The Circle of Enlightenment." It is a circle that is hand drawn in one or two brushstrokes to express a moment when the mind is free to let the body create. Some artists draw the Ensō as an open circle, while other compete the circle. Ensō symbolizes many things: strength, elegance, the universe, our true and innermost self, beauty in imperfection, and the oneness of all things in life.

www.ingramcontent.com/pod-product-compliance
Lightning Source LLC
Chambersburg PA
CBHW051342040426
42453CB00007B/369